LOOK TO THE LAND

LORD NORTHBOURNE

LOOK TO
THE LAND

SOPHIA PERENNIS

HILLSDALE NY

Second, revised special edition 2003
First edition, J.M. Dent & Sons, 1940, 1942

For information, address:
Sophia Perennis, P.O. Box 611
Hillsdale NY 12529
www.sophiaperennis.com

Printed in the
United States of America

Library of Congress Cataloging-in-Publication Data

Northbourne, Lord, 1896–1982
Look to the land / Lord Northbourne.—second, rev. ed.

p.   cm.
ISBN 0 900588 89 6 (pbk. : alk. paper)
ISBN 1 59731 018 2 (cloth: alk. paper)
1. Organic farming. 2. Agricultural Ecology.
3. Agriculture—Social aspects. I. Title.
S 605.5 N 68 2003
631.5'84—dc22   2003027275

CONTENTS

✠

Walter James, the fourth Lord Northbourne, wrote this book in 1938–1939. It was first published in 1940, when the storm clouds of war had already closed over England. During the previous fifteen years he had developed one of the first 'organic' estates in England. Both farm and garden were run on the Biodynamic principles laid down by Rudolf Steiner.

I hope that the republishing of this book may make some contribution to the current debate about organic farming, and to that other debate about revitalizing local communities.

CHRISTOPHER JAMES
5th LORD NORTHBOURNE

FOREWORD

'Without vision the people perish.' So wrote the poet William Blake. Lord Northbourne (1896–1982) was a man of excep-tional vision, who diagnosed the sickness of modern society as stemming from the severance of its organic links with the whole-ness of life. Northbourne's early advocacy of organic agriculture (he is said to have coined the term) was joined to a deep conviction that humanity does not live by bread alone, and that the fullness of human life demands obedience to sacred law. Like his better-known younger contemporary E. F. Schumacher (influential author of *Small is Beautiful*), whose work developed along similar lines, his vision of life came to embrace fully the interrelationship of God, humanity, and the soil as a unity presupposing a way of life in stark contrast to that of the myopic, mechanistic world he saw encroach-ing on all sides. And so, as it becomes more and more evident that such a way of life stands to imperil our very future and that of the delicate ecosystem on which all life depends, it is time to re-examine the work of this pioneering thinker, whose vision of what is required by a truly meaningful and sustainable society embraced traditional metaphysics, religion, farming, the arts, the rural crafts, and mone-tary reform.

After serving in WWI, Lord Northbourne took an agricultural degree at Oxford, and taught there in the 1920s. In 1932 he took over management of the family seat near Deal, in Kent, implementing biodynamic farming methods throughout the estate and gardens. A highly cultured man who applied himself to painting and horti-culture, he was fully engaged with the agricultural issues of his day, serving after WWII as chairman both of the Kent Agricultural Exec-utive Committee and the Wye Agricultural College. His view that mankind mediates between God and Nature through the art of husbandry led Northbourne to write on the many wider social and economic implications of environmental damage in a unique way that has not been equalled in the intervening years (Wendell Berry perhaps comes closest in spirit), and so Sophia Perennis has undertaken also to publish revised and updated editions of Lord Northbourne's two other works, *Religion in the Modern World* and *Looking Back on Progress*. A fourth volume of collected essays is in prepartion. These later works present his wider reflections on the Divine and human society, but always with the sensibility of a man who has roots in the soil. He corresponded with Thomas Merton, as well as mountaineer and Tibetan Buddhist Marco Pallis (*The Way and the Mountain*), who introduced him to the school of perennialist writers. Northbourne translated René Guénon's *The Reign of Quantity and the Signs of the Times*, described by renowned comparative religionist Huston Smith as one of the truly seminal books of the twentieth century, as well as Frithjof Schuon's *Light on Ancient Worlds* and Titus Burckhardt's *Sacred Art in East and West*. He was also a frequent contributor to the British periodical *Studies in Comparative Religion*, which in his final years Schumacher recommended as one of the most important journals in English.

Lord Northbourne had a special gift for expressing the profoundest truths in simple and graceful language—without however ever 'popularizing'. And his work, first published more than 60 years ago, was so remarkably prescient that only now, perhaps, are more profound ecological thinkers approaching the point where his deep metaphysical insights can begin to fructify their work. It is the publisher's hope, then, that Lord Northbourne's unique combination of gentleness and rigor will spur a new generation of readers to engage the burning issues of our day with some measure of the compassion, artistic sensitivity, and intellect he possessed.

CHAPTER ONE

The interdependence of living creatures—the organism not a machine—farming a part of every man's life—the soil a living entity—the nutritional needs of plants—the importance of humus—erosion the death of the soil—the extent of erosion—the causes of erosion, physical and economic—international debt—financial and biological cost—the urge to speed—concentration of population—the state of British farming

EVERY DETAIL OF THE LIFE OF EVERY MAN is in some way related to the lives of innumerable other people, and is dependent on them; the people concerned are mostly quite unknown to him, and may be living almost anywhere on the surface of the earth. Though this be a truism, it must be stated in order to emphasize the uselessness of considering the situation of any man or association of men or geographical unit as if it were isolated from all others. It must also be stated in order to be extended.

Besides being bound up with the lives of his fellow men, every man's life is bound up with the lives of innumerable non-human creatures which constitute his food, which provide him with clothing, shelter, material to work with, or pleasure; and to whose lives he in turn consciously or unconsciously contributes. Thus there is a very real economic and biological linkage, comprehensive and of infinite complexity, between all living creatures in the world. This linkage really constitutes the lives of those creatures. With the improvement in communications accompanying the progress of the mechanical age, this linkage has become more comprehensive, more rapid, and more direct than it ever was before between parts of the world physically remote from each other. This fact is clearly recognized as an important feature of the economic situation. But the economic aspect of things, being largely concerned with the production of food and raw materials from animals and plants, is clearly a function of biological states. Economics have been discussed *ad nauseam*. The biological state of the world has, in its broader aspects, received relatively little attention, though it conditions the economic state.

Above all these matters is the spiritual aspect of the relationships which constitute the life of man. It is said that man is a spiritual being. He may not always be so, but at least his existence is valuable only in proportion to its spirituality. He can achieve spirituality only if earthly things are not his masters: only if he can control the earthly side of his being, thereby achieving that perfect balance which alone permits of higher development. That which is sick is out of control, and is upsetting the balance. The spiritual sickness of the world is, like the economic sickness, very rightly a matter of profound concern. These, together with the biological sickness which is the subject of this book, are almost certainly only different aspects of one phenomenon. But that is no reason to ignore the biological view of the situation, which must always for us, while we are alive, be a very relevant view. In taking it we can and must try to relate it to other concerns—economic, intellectual, and spiritual.

Biology is the study of the mechanism of life, and this mechanism is a continuous flow of matter through the architectural forms we know as organisms. The form alone has any life or any organic identity, just as a whirlpool has identity, though it has no continuity of substance. So there can be no true analogy between even the simplest living creature and any conceivable machine. The said flow of matter is the process of nutrition in its widest aspects. Each kind of organism obtains the continuous supply of material which it needs for its nutrition in its own characteristic way. Most of the higher forms of life can only use material which has been previously taken up by other (not necessarily lower) forms of life, and which at the time of use retains the architecture of those other forms. Man is, of course, absolutely dependent on the availability of material of that kind for his nutrition, and, as is the case with other creatures, only a limited category of such material is suited to his particular needs. Man, being omnivorous, has a wider range of choice than most.

Man used to get what he needed by hunting. Then he discovered the arts of cultivation, and a very great increase in his numbers became possible. Farming (including for the sake of brevity now and hereafter every kind of cultivation of crops or animals) became his only possible way of maintaining life: it became not only necessarily his main occupation, but also the critical link in that flow of material which is himself, and a link dependent for its soundness on his own efforts. That which links together all the phases and processes of farming, and which is therefore its foundation, is the soil in all its infinite variety. If the soil is the foundation of farming, the soil is also the foundation of the physical life of man. It is the background of his life. The importance of farming in the national life is now receiving wider recognition. But that recognition mostly takes the form of a vague realization that the most is not being made of a national asset, one valuable in peace and indispensable in war, and that the 6 per cent or so of the population of Britain which is actively engaged in farming is in a very difficult position. Most of the consideration given to farming in this country is based upon that very limited point of view. It is assumed that farming is one of the many activities which are of importance in the national life, and that we are only interested in farming in other countries insofar as they may be able to produce food more cheaply than we can. Such agitation as is directed to the improvement of farming in Britain mostly comes from the 6 per cent who work on the land, and thus from so small a minority that it could not be effective even if it were wisely directed and free from suspicion of sectional prejudice. Few people realize as yet that the agricultural problem is by its very nature very bit as much a townsman's problem as it is a farmer's problem: and that there is far more in it than a question of cheap and abundant supplies food.

This book is an attempt by a layman, writing for laymen, to set forth how much more there is in it. It is an attempt at a biological and economic conspectus of our present situation. As such, it must start from the soil.

First, as to the nature of soil. Each of the innumerable kinds of soil can be looked at as a complex of variables, living and non-living, quite staggering in the number and variety of its factors. Many of these factors have been the objects of scientific study, both separately and in combination. Many valuable and learned books have been written about them. There is certainly no end to this kind of study of the soil. Sir E. J. Russell's *Soil Conditions and Plant Growth* is an excellent introduction to it. The soil is a whole world to itself. But as a world it is also an entity: a variable entity and a living entity, and one with which, as an entity, every farmer and gardener is intimately concerned. Most people in the world are still farmers or gardeners, and they, who handle the soil, must look upon it and treat it as a living whole. For it is as a living thing, not as a dead medium, that the soil is most important to us.

Before proceeding to a further justification of that statement, it may be well to discuss the impression that plants need dead minerals only for their full development. That impression is widely held, even among people who cultivate plants. It is a result of forming generalizations, which are probably premature, from scientific findings about the mineral requirements of plants. These findings are valid so far as they go, but they do not contain the whole truth. Among these findings is the established fact that plants can be grown in pure water containing nothing but minerals in solution: or on sterilized sand supplied with such water. The growing of plants in this way has become quite a common procedure, not only in laboratories, but even on a commercial scale. The Americans have christened the process with the name of 'hydroponics', and a great future has been predicted for it. The chief advantage seems to be that, the medium being sterile, it is easier to avoid diseases caused or conveyed by living organisms.

It is premature to attempt to assess the future commercial importance of the fact that plants can be grown successfully on entirely non-living media. It is, even more premature, and far more foolish, to assert that because this is so it is no longer necessary to consider the soil as if it were anything but a non-living medium through which the necessary chemicals can be supplied to plants. Yet this assertion has been made; and more, it has even been treated as an assumption in practice. The disastrous results which have in fact followed this assumption are dealt with at length hereafter. Meanwhile it may be observed that plants can only grow on a non-living medium if all the chemical compounds they need are supplied, and if the physical condition of the medium as regards aeration, etc., is suitable. These conditions are difficult to fulfill except on a small scale. Therefore plants grown by hydroponic methods or their equivalent are not likely to supply man with a significant fraction of his needs for a long time to come, if ever. For all practical purposes we must continue to rely almost entirely on our soil as we find it. And as we find it, it is not a bit like an establishment for hydroponic culture, nor can it be made so. It will be a long time before the true status of hydroponics is established. Meanwhile it is at least legitimate to hold the view that better results can be achieved by less artificial methods, quite apart from the practical necessity of continuing those methods for an indefinite period.

A valid test of the ultimate significance of hydroponics would be very difficult and expensive and would take a long time. For its ultimate significance depends on the quality of the product, and that is a very subtle matter involving something more than appearance and taste, and more than chemical composition as revealed by analysis. That 'something' may be described as 'effectiveness as a vehicle of life.' If that effectiveness is to be established experimentally it must be tested in at least two ways. Firstly, a considerable number of generations of plants must be cultivated by hydroponic methods alone. If no progressive loss of vigor is shown, the second test can be proceeded with. This involves the feeding of animals on the produce of this isolated hydroponic cultivation only, and here again the work must be carried on through a number of generations of animals. The whole system must be nutritionally completely isolated throughout the experiment. Practical considerations might preclude the choice of man himself as the animal concerned, though that choice would be the ideal one. No less ambitious experiment will serve, yet if proper scientific control is to be provided at all stages the enterprise assumes alarming proportions.

Perhaps we need not worry too much about it, for if we are to understand life and its needs, we shall not do so by cutting it up and looking at each bit separately. A controlled experiment involving the whole of life is impossible, but attaining a broader view of life, one which is synthetic rather than analytic, is not impossible.

All this is in defence of the assertion that it is as a living entity, not as a dead medium, that the soil is important to us. If the reader is not yet convinced of this, he is still invited to read on.

It is the top layer of the soil which is alive; that layer which may be from an inch or two to a foot or two in depth, and which is, in general, darker in color and more friable than any of the layers lower down which constitute the subsoil. There is no need to tell farmers or gardeners that plants grow readily in the top soil, and will only grow very badly, if at all, in subsoil; though the subsoil is often richer in minerals. The top layer is darker and more friable because it contains 'humus'. Humus is a product of the decay of once living material. Decay is of course a biological process—it does not occur in the absence of organisms—and humus itself exhibits varying degrees of biological activity. It is the great controlling and balancing factor in the soil. The suitability of a soil for cultivation depends to some extent on the nature and conditions of its mineral constituents, but more on the humus it contains: both as to the amount of that humus, which can vary from zero to nearly one hundred per cent, and still more as to the state of activity of the humus. A pure peat is nearly 100 per cent humus; but most of it is inactive, so it is infertile. The depth and activity of the living layer is the measure of the fertility of a soil.

This layer has other characteristics besides color and relative crumbliness. Humus, the balancer, can not only make sticky soils crumbly, it can also give cohesion to soils which would otherwise be too friable, for instance to sandy soil. It improves the 'tilth' of all soils. A soil in good tilth absorbs and retains water, yet it allows any surplus to pass through it. Unless the passage of such water is obstructed lower down, such a soil never becomes waterlogged; yet it suffers less from drought than a similar soil not in good tilth. It acts like a sponge: greedy for all it can comfortably carry, and retentive of it, but allowing any surplus to escape. If the humus in a soil is lost or becomes inactive, the soil will gradually lose these characteristics and revert to its inherent faults: stickiness, dryness, or whatever they may be.

These facts are well established and easily verified. The other main characteristic of the living layer is the basis of most sound practice, but is much less easy to test scientifically. Therefore these days its importance is underestimated. It is so inconvenient when things will not submit to exact measurement that we prefer to ignore them even if, as in this case, they are vital. The characteristic is that of acting upon the minerals in the soil and rendering them available to plants; or, to put the point in a more obscure yet probably not less valid way, the conferring on plants of the power to make use of minerals in the soil, even though these be present only in excessively minute quantities. There is no doubt that in practice when the biological activity of the soil falls, plants growing in it begin to show symptoms of specific deficiencies; sometimes even when chemical analysis reveals no lack of the particular constituent concerned. That constituent is then said to be present in a form in which it is not available to plants, and is added to the soil in chemical form. The extreme case is that of the hydroponics already mentioned, in which the plant is growing on a non-living medium, and all requirements have to be supplied artificially in exactly the right form and proportions. How many so-called soil deficiencies are really due to non-activity of the living layer of the soil? To attempt an answer now would be to anticipate unduly.

So when the living layer loses activity—but let us not prevaricate any longer and start that sentence again. When the living layer is sickly or dying the soil loses its tilth or texture, its control of water, and its powers of digestion, That is to say, it loses its fertility. So loss of fertility is the ill health of the soil. The soil becomes unhealthy when the living layer is not supplied with the right food. That food is, broadly speaking, organic matter in the right state of decay, or in condition to undergo such decay.

In the later stages of ill health, the top layer of the soil changes in accordance with the nature of its mineral constituents. It may become hard, so that not only can roots not penetrate it, but rain runs off the surface without sinking in. Such hard soil tends to crack. The rain runs in the cracks, which widen into gullies. These gullies finally coalesce and the whole surface may be washed away. That is one kind of erosion, or death of the soil. Alternatively, the surface may become very loose. In that condition it can be washed away; but it is also liable to be caught and blown away by the wind. Thus can a once fertile soil not only be totally lost, but converted to an instrument of destruction: silting up rivers and causing floods, or choking living creatures with dust. Erosion can be slow or rapid. Soil can be washed slowly downhill on sloping land, gradually impoverishing the higher or more sloping ground—so-called sheet erosion. But, fast or slow, the end is the same: the sea, whence geological upheavals alone can recover the lost soil.

Much of the soil which is moved in the course of erosion does not reach the sea for a very long time, if at all. When it is water-borne it forms deposits in valleys or in deltas which are known as alluvium. When it is wind-borne the deposits are known as loess. Alluvium and loess provide some of the most fertile soils known. The fact that some of the best soils in the world consist of deposits which are the result of erosion elsewhere might lead to the supposition that erosion does not matter much when it amounts merely to a transfer of soil from one land area to another. But that supposition is a serious mistake, for several reasons. For if you double the depth of a soil, it is only in very exceptional circumstances that you will get double the crop per unit of area. In other words, if you super-imposed all the soil from one acre of cultivated ground on that of a neighboring acre, you would almost certainly not be able to grow as much as you could before on the two acres. Also, there is a limit to the useful depth of a soil, which varies according to the crops to be grown, but may be said never to exceed a few feet at most. Some loess soils are several hundred feet deep. Only the top foot or two is available; the rest is once fertile soil which has been buried. Again, much of the soil deposited by water is often largely subsoil; in the case of wind erosion it is often sand or dust which has become erodible because it has lost its fertility. Though such deposits may be potentially fertile, it takes a long time for them to become so. In the meantime they can, and often do, bury a mature fertile soil to such a depth that its accumulated fertility is rendered inaccessible, and ultimately destroyed from lack of aeration. So it will be seen that it is only in very exceptional circumstances that movements of soil are advantageous, even to the soil which receives the deposit; only in fact when the deposit is very thin and even and consists of fully weathered and potentially active material. The eroded soil always loses. It may be hazarded that there is hardly ever a net gain as a result of such movements, and usually a loss extending over both the eroded and the receiving area.

Erosion is always going on, even on some soils which are in a good state of fertility. It begins to matter when the rate of erosion exceeds the rate at which life can invade the mineral rock underlying the soil and convert it into soil. That rate is variable, but always very slow; of the order of one inch in 500 to 1,000 years. It matters desperately when the rate of erosion mounts up to very much higher rates than that, as it often does. A high erosion rate in a few limited areas would be regrettable; but when it covers whole continents, as it does today, the fate of the world, and of man with it, must be hanging in the balance. It is very difficult to form a scientifically reliable estimate of the real extent, of erosion; but there is enough evidence to show that its incidence is world-wide and severe. No country is wholly exempt, but the big continental areas are generally the most seriously affected. There is a fairly large and growing amount of literature on the subject. Probably the most comprehensive survey is *The Rape of the Earth* by Jacks and Whyte.

The country which has received most attention in this connection is the U.S.A., and deservedly so, for America as usual is out for records. Alarming statistics can be quoted endlessly. On 56.4 per cent of the land surface of the U.S.A., a quarter or more of the soil has been lost. The total loss of fertility has been estimated at 30 to 50 per cent of the total originally available. 'The amount of soil annually reaching the sea is between 500 and 1,000 million tons, representing 2,000 million dollars' worth of plant food, or twenty-one times the amount annually removed in crops; but that represents only a fraction of the total damage. Fifteen million acres have been totally destroyed, but this is 'an insignificant part of the story, for it is the less violent forms of wastage—sheet erosion—which is doing the bulk of the damage to the land.' The Missouri basin has lost an average of seven inches of top soil in twenty-four years. (Professor Chamberlin has estimated the mean rate of soil formation as only one inch in 10,000 years.) In California and elsewhere the new deserts are called 'dust-bowls'. The biggest one has advanced in places as much as forty miles in one year, destroying 2,500 farms.

Efforts to stop it by tree planting, etc., have failed. The grazing lands of the West are not exempt, for over-grazing and fires have removed the natural cover. Obviously every other problem with which America is faced sinks into insignificance in comparison with this one. It is already too late to do more than save something from the wreck.

Much the same is true of many other countries. Australia is probably going faster than America, but has only been under 'civilized' influence for one-third of the period. Over-stocking and unsound cultural methods are the chief troubles there; there is much gully erosion. The wheat-lands of New South Wales are said to be getting visibly worse each year.

In Africa, the Sahara desert is moving southward at a mean rate of over half a mile a year, the Turkana desert eastward at six or seven miles a year. But the whole continent is suffering from erosion in every known form, the extension of deserts and the creation of new ones. It is well known that Kenya is rapidly becoming infertile and is beginning to suffer from locusts. This is no new phenomenon in Africa, for it is known that the northern Sahara was once the granary of Rome, and it is believed that in Roman times the Congo forest reached nearly to Khartoum, from which it is now separated by 1,500 miles of desert or semi-desert. Erosion is not new, perhaps, but the whole process has been enormously accelerated in the last few years.

China presents remarkable contrasts between the best and the worst. Some of the best cultivation in the world is practised over extensive areas (see Professor King's classic *Farmers of Forty Centuries*), yet over areas far more extensive the worst types of erosion prevail. The well-cultivated areas are by no means all immune from its effects. Chinese industry and care for the land is unequalled, yet it cannot prevent the periodical destruction caused by the Yellow River floods. This river alone carries down 2,500 million tons of eroded soil a year, equal to one foot on 2,000 square miles. Its bed gets silted up between embankments, which must be constantly raised till its bed is well above the surrounding land. Nothing can save that land or its people when an embankment bursts. All that is largely because fuel is scarce in China and the hills have been denuded to provide it. In this way what was once the hunting-ground of Genghis Khan has been turned into the Gobi desert.

In Russia erosion on a serious scale has been going on for a long time, though no reliable estimate of its extent seems to be available. The important feature there is that it has been very greatly accelerated by the much-vaunted large-scale mechanical cultivation which has been introduced in recent years. Russia, with her vast areas of low rainfall and high winds, may be well on the way to rivalling America as record-holder in rapidity and extent of desert formation.

In Canada, South America, and India the same tendencies are observable in varying incidence, with, so far as can be seen, no compensating tendency towards increase of fertility. Increase of production must not be confused with increase of fertility. Increased production for human use can be and usually is secured by cashing in on existing fertility and using it up, with the disastrous effects described.

Most of the land area of the world has now been mentioned, with the exception of Europe. In Europe actual erosion has not occurred on a spectacular scale. Nevertheless it is known, for instance, that in Greece the hill tops were once forests and the slopes were covered with soil and grass. They are not so today. It is also known that there has been a progressive desiccation of the soil in the whole Mediterranean region during at least the past 300 years. Terraced cultivation used to be more prevalent and more carefully maintained than is the case today, and forests have been destroyed for fuel. There is reason to suppose that the washing down of hill sides is proceeding in places at a dangerous rate; for instance, in Savoy at least 100,000 acres of good land have been spoilt by coarse silt deposited on them during floods. In England the blowing away of certain of the light fen soils has attracted attention recently.

But serious erosion is only the culminating stage of a process of which the initial stage is usually loss of fertility of some kind. Loss of fertility is vastly more extensive in its incidence than erosion. A picture of the extent of erosion gives merely an indication of the much greater incidence of loss of fertility. If erosion represents the death of the soil, and is as extensive as it appears to be, how much land is part-way towards death? The question would be pertinent if the rate of erosion were steady. But it is not steady, it is increasing very rapidly almost all over the world. Probably more soil has been lost since 1914 than in the whole previous history of the world.

This is not a 'natural' phenomenon in the ordinary sense of the word. There cannot be any doubt that so far as the modern growth of deserts is concerned it is not nature but man who is the desert maker. It is not unlikely that most of the great deserts of the world are of his making. When we consider how he sets about it now in conjunction with the fact that traces of high civilization are found in many areas now desert, the probability of his past guilt becomes greater. And the exhaustion of the fertility of the soil is no new thing, nor is the temptation to practise it for immediate gain. The new feature in the situation is that man has recently enormously extended his physical powers by the use of mechanical devices. One man can now do what used to be the work of dozens or even hundreds, and can do it faster.

Natural erosion is either very slow; or, where it is relatively rapid, it occurs only under special conditions, such as are found on high and barren mountains. Nor does a high rate of erosion necessarily accompany cultivation. Some areas, for instance parts of China, have been highly cultivated for at least 4,000 years without loss of fertility, and probably with an accretion of fertile soil rather than with a loss of soil.

Man sets about his desert-making in various ways. He alters the texture of the soil by using up humus and failing to replace it—by failing to feed the soil with organic matter; livestock are the great converters of otherwise unwanted organic matter to a form in which it can be used by plants. Stockless farming, understocking, burning straw, etc., are all cases of failure to observe the 'Rule of Return' which is the essence of farming. Only by faithfully returning to the soil in due course everything that has come from it can fertility be made permanent and the earth be made to yield a genuine increase.

Large-scale monoculture (the growing of one crop only) upsets the balance of factors in the soil in many ways. There is no give and take between crops. Disease spreads easily. Nature always provides a mixture of plants, and of animals; only so can living matter be kept constantly in circulation without wastage.

In warm countries especially, over-exposure of the soil to air and light and heat by injudicious cultivation may lead to so rapid a decay of humus that a minimum amount cannot be maintained in the soil. This is the source of so-called tropical erosion.

A fruitful cause of erosion, usually in combination with one or more of those already listed, is the direct exposure of the soil to the forces of wind and water by removal of natural cover, either by clearing and burning, or by the plough alone, or by over-stocking, or by ill-judged stocking (especially with goats), or by introducing destructive animals such as rabbits; together with failure to provide alternative cover or properly adjusted periods of rest for the recovery of natural vegetation. Alternative cover can be provided by crops, especially varied crops grown in rotation or in strips, and sometimes hedges or shelter belts. Into this category of causes comes deforestation. The injudicious felling of timber may lead to much more than denudation the hills on which the timber grows. Forests act as sponges, and level out the rate at which water leaves the hills. Thus injudicious deforestation leads to erosion on the hills, and to alternations of flood and drought in the valleys, ending in erosion or harmful silting of the valleys themselves.

The last category into which man's destructive activities fall is that of the injudicious cultivation of sloping land. This, again, may occur in combination with other factors. Soil will always move down a slope, even a slight one, unless that slope is terraced, especially on arable land. It is surprising how quickly the soil piles up on one side of a permanent footpath or hedge in arable land, and drops away on the other. Such erosion may or may not be serious. It can only be prevented by horizontal terracing, such as has been practised from time immemorial by all good cultivators. It can be greatly accelerated, up to the point at which it becomes disastrous, by cultivating sloping land in unduly big fields and by drawing furrows up and down instead of across the slope.

This is not a complete list of the causes of erosion. In various combinations they lead to the drying out and blowing away of the soil, or to its being washed away; evenly in sheet erosion, unevenly when gullies are formed. That is how deserts are made. Once started, they grow. Blowing sand smothers vegetation at the edges. When rain falls there is no surface sponge to regulate its flow, so plants, animals, and men are killed or driven away and sheets of subsoily mud are spread over fertile soil by floods which are followed by parching drought. And then the locusts come.

In comparison with the speed at which soil is being lost all over the world, relatively very little has yet been done to mitigate the evil. The speed, however, tends to increase in geometrical rather than in arithmetical progression, and some awareness of the gravity of the situation has been forced upon certain peoples in recent years, particularly on the people of the U.S.A. Even in that country the problem has not yet taken the place which it must take in the attention of the people and their government if the speed of loss is to be stabilized—in the near future—let alone materially reduced. Nevertheless there is hope there that quite a big proportion of the American continent may ultimately be preserved in a permanently habitable state, though in one much reduced from its former richness. The same cannot be said with confidence of any other badly eroded area—perhaps least of all of Africa and Australia.

Erosion is nearly all man's work. Some of it can be attributed to mere foolishness. But most of it is due to greed combined with the existence of the possibility of 'getting rich quick' by exhausting the land and underselling competitors. But the actual tillers of the soil who have got rich are few. What then has been the inducement to so many to despoil the land on which they depend for a living, and to despoil it within the last century or so to a hitherto unheard-of extent? What has been the stimulus to the rapid extension of exhaustive farming all over the world?

The stimulus has been a great development of the said possibilities of getting rich quickly, a development partly dependent on the evolution of new and powerful machines, and partly on a roughly simultaneous world-wide extension of a peculiar economic system, which has led to a vast accumulation of financial debt. Such debt, both internal and international, has grown to a point at which repayment is generally out of the question, and the payment of interest alone has become severely oppressive. The only way any one can pay this interest is by producing or manufacturing and selling something with a view to making a money profit out of which to pay it. So purely financial considerations have everywhere acquired dominance over all others. The nature of this dominance can best be shown by a simple illustration of the working of the system on the grand scale. This illustration is chosen because it has particular application to the situation under discussion, in which the actual wealth in the soil of one country is exploited and exhausted for the supposed benefit of another country. International debt and soil erosion are twin brother and sister, inseparables. But international debts are not the only debts which may become cumulative and oppressive to the point of leaving the debtor no alternative but to exhaust his resources and himself in attempts to keep going, let alone to extricate himself from their toils. The street-corner moneylender and his client stand in much the same relationship to each other as do the bondholder in the imaginary country hereafter called A and the farmer in country B. In each case it is to the lender's advantage that the borrower should not get out of debt; in each case he must persuade both himself and the borrower that the arrangement is one for mutual benefit; in each case, however, the final exhaustion of the borrower is bound to leave the lender himself with nothing for the future, whatever he may be supposed to have gained during the currency of the loan.

Consider the case of an international loan made by country A to country B to enable B to 'develop'. (A expects both orders from B and interest on the loan.) B could pay interest on the loan in gold, if she could spare enough. If she cannot produce the gold B *must* sell goods to A or to some other country to get the money with which to pay A (unless, as often happens, she borrows the money to pay with from A; but that increases the debt). B must sell those goods or default on payments, which she can't afford to do; even if she has to sell at a loss (or, what is the same thing, subsidize her exporters). A does not like this, because it undercuts her home prices. So she puts on tariffs and takes other steps to restrict imports. But countries C, D, E, F, etc., are in similar positions: fighting to cut prices outside or maintain internal ones, or both, to get a 'favorable' balance of trade or reduce an 'adverse' balance. Now countries in B's position are *ex hypothesi* 'undeveloped'. They have areas of virgin or unoccupied land. By despoiling this land of its fertility they can produce food very cheaply. Those inhabitants of A who are the holders of B's bonds will welcome this because (1) they get their interest; (2) cheap food enables them to cut manufacturing costs; (3) the cry of cheap food is political jam for any one who sees a profit in the system. So B's land is ruined—and so is A's because of the cut prices of food; but nobody who matters seems to mind that much. It is not noticed that 'development' has destroyed the one inalienable and potentially inexhaustible source of wealth of both: till, perhaps, too late.

It will be observed that this situation arises only in connection with the payment of interest on loans. Repayment of any part of the principal is wholly out of the question, except by substituting a new loan for the old one, but, of course that does not reduce the debt. Conversion is common enough, and so are repudiation or failure. Repayment is very rare.

So the possibility of carrying on without upheaval has come to depend on ability to undercut competitors in the world's markets. The only way to do that is to 'rationalize' production, which involves capital expenditure on machinery and plant, which again necessitates the borrowing of money. So debt grows.

The term 'rationalization' is a rather vague one. It always implies in the end the employment of less labour to achieve a desired result, and the attainment of that result in a shorter time; briefly, a reduction of financial cost. Financial costs have been much studied recently, and a lot is known about them. But the relation of financial cost to what may be termed 'biological cost' has not been considered, still less estimated. Biological cost may be translated 'ultimate effect on vitality.' The necessity for inventing a term for the statement of the problem is sufficient proof that it has not been tackled. For one thing there has not been time—for it would be long-range work. Luckily, a statistical survey is not the only means of arriving at wisdom.

Rationalization implies in the end mainly an increase of speed. Its object is that the same number of men should produce more in a given time. In applying it we forget that life is a rhythmical process. 'The music of the spheres' is no mere poetic phrase. It is reflected in the life-processes of all creatures, and of their associations, and not only so in such obvious physical phenomena as the seasons, the tides, the alternations of night and day, the beating of a heart, or the finer vibrations studied by physicists. The harmonious rhythms of life are thrown into discord by the inexorable urge to speed and ever more speed which is the inevitable accompaniment of a way of life dominated by the mathematical fiction which we know as money. He who doubts the reality of that dominance should ask any farmer who has weeds in his fields why he allows them to grow there, and also whether it is really for the good of his farm that they should be allowed to grow.

It is, however, not debt accumulation alone from which our farms suffer, though that may reach fantastic limits. For instance, the ascertained debts of Australian farmers, exclusive of private debt, exceed in total the value of their entire assets, including stock, crops, and the land itself. Such a situation is merely fantastic; it is meaningless because those assets are obviously unrealizable in the circumstances. (How curious it is that we 'realize' when we mean 'sell' or now use the word 'turn into money'. Thus do we mistake the shadow for the substance.) There is another complication. It is the fact that our economic and financial system has an inherent instability. For hundreds of years farm prices have fluctuated wildly. Short booms have been followed by long slumps. The mechanism of this instability is the mutual interaction of prices and the circulation of bank credit (that is to say, of the rate and volume of borrowing), which act together on the psychological factor known to financiers as confidence. These factors mutually reinforce each other until 'overborrowing' occurs, that is to say till credit is so far expanded that there is a danger that demands on the cash reserve of the banks may exceed the safety limit. This reserve is by custom kept at about 10 per cent of liabilities. When this happens the banks have to call in loans, or issue fewer than are repaid, so contracting credit and lowering prices. The result is then that the mutual interaction, through confidence, of prices and credit, operates in a reverse direction and all three collapse together.

One other factor is of first importance in this situation. It is that the cash reserve of the banks, which limits the volume of borrowing, has hitherto been related to the amount of gold held by the banks. This amount bears no relation to the volume of world production, and especially of world harvests, which vary seasonally. The value of

world agricultural production greatly exceeds that of all other production. So a big world harvest, or still more a series of such, means
more food but not more money, and consequently a fall in farm
prices. But most people in the world are still working on the land.
The purchasing power of such people amounts to about 70 per cent
of the world's total. If farm prices fall, the purchasing power of 70
per cent of the world's population falls, and industrialists lose their
main market. So industrial prices then fall, and with them, confidence. Slump conditions then prevail, with their accompaniment of
unemployment and unsalable surpluses of goods.

Instability of prices, when it goes beyond a certain point, takes
away whatever chance the farmer might have of coping with the
competition with which he is faced. For the farmer's main job is
the steady building up of the fertility of the soil; a job quite incompatible with constant changes of policy, forced upon him by changes
in the price situation.

Under present conditions the only thing that pays is quick profit-
making while the going is good. By ignorant or unscrupulous
exploitation and exhaustion of fertility vast profits have been made
(by financiers rather than by farmers) in the name of cheap food.
The pace is forced for the sound farmer wherever he lives. The time
factor becomes ever more and more important, as every one has to
snatch at the chances of the moment to catch up with the accumulation of debt, and achieve a quick turnover to minimize overhead
costs per unit of production. If what has been said about the state of
farming in the world is true, there is no need to dwell at length on
the importance to mankind of a relaxation of the inexorable urge to
speed under which both man and the land on which he lives are
exhausted. As is usual nowadays, it will be left to future generations
to pay for our mistakes, but they may not have the wherewithal.
Money alone is notoriously useless in a desert.

The same causes underlie the curious maldistribution of population from which the world suffers. All countries have suffered from
'surpluses' of goods which they cannot sell at a remunerative price,
and unemployed people whom they cannot pay; including so-called
undeveloped or newly developed countries, which consequently
have very soon found themselves unable to absorb any more people.

A large part of the world's population is concentrated in thickly populated countries, and within each country a large and increasing proportion of the people are concentrated in towns. These are not two separate phenomena, but one only. The towns suck the life out of the country, and gain nothing in the process but money. Similarly, countries with concentrated populations suck the life out of their colonies before those colonies are even partially developed. New Zealand, for instance, with an area about equal to, and with potentialities at least approaching, those of Great Britain, has a population of about one and one-third millions, as against the latter's forty-five millions. Yet the unoccupied, or unsatisfactorily occupied, people in this country can no more go and assist in the development of New Zealand than can the inhabitants of London find satisfactory opportunities in the country. It is true that New Zealand has less in the way of natural resources than Britain, especially in coal and minerals, so that she might not be fitted to support quite so big a population. Nevertheless, the present disproportion is fantastic. Not less so are the many other artificial concentrations of people all over the world. Parts of the world are far too full, while others equally suitable for habitation remain underpopulated simply because it does not pay to populate them. However much it would be for the good of mankind to do so, the money is not forthcoming. The people must go where the money goes; to the place towards which money gravitates, not to the place where the goods are, nor where the goods could be most advantageously produced, nor where they themselves could live most happily if exchange of goods and services were allowed to proceed naturally.

So while there is room and ample room for millions more people in the colonies, and in rural areas, the people in fact must stay in the mother country and in the centers of population, which steal away from the country its fertility and the people who could restore that fertility. Those people might find their souls in doing so, and in doing so they might revive the towns.

Now let us look closer and see in more detail how the land of this country has been affected. Nobody who has ever seen land decently cultivated, who goes about with his eyes open, needs any help from statistics in arriving at a view of the lamentable condition of much of our land. It is generally admitted that the reserves of fertility used up during the war of 1914–18 have not been replaced. The downward tendency began before that, but since the war the fall has been more rapid. Much of the less naturally fertile land has gone nearly or quite out of cultivation. The rural population is still steadily falling; add to which the alarming fact that, of the male workers on the land, disproportionately few are between the ages of twenty-five and forty-five. There are huge areas, especially in the North and West, where the population is one-third or less of what it used to be. These areas once were prosperous mixed farms with a considerable proportion of arable on the lower ground. Now they have no arable land and only carry a few sheep, and those increasingly sickly. Two million acres have been taken from our farms for other purposes since the war. Of the remainder, Sir George Stapledon has estimated that 43 per cent is in a state which he describes as 'deplorable', while being at the same time from the technical point of view easily improvable.

It is true that our total agricultural production has slightly increased during the past decade. This increase has come almost entirely from the best land, much of which is in a state of high pro-ductivity. There is increasing concentration on such land. But does this mean that all our land might be, according to its natural fertility, relatively equally productive? It does not—for three reasons. The first is that there would be a very big increase of production, and the prices of most farm products would fall, making it impossible to maintain the hypothetical universal high standard. Why! even now we find it necessary to restrict the production of many articles of food in order to maintain their prices. The second reason is that imports of food would in the end have to be reduced, which might be bad business for our shipowners and for the holders of foreign bonds, who rely for the payment of interest on what remains of their bonds, whether they know it or not, and mainly on the money paid for food imported into this country. The exporting or debtor coun-try can of course pay in no other way, for reasons which have been explained. The third reason for which the productivity of all our land could not imitate that of the most productive, at least for more than a short time, is more subtle. But it is far the most important reason in the end. It is a real one and not merely a financial one. It is as follows:

The productivity of much of our highly farmed land is dependent on the feeding to animals of imported feeding stuffs and on the application of artificial manures to the land, most of which are imported. The world supply of artificial manures, especially of phosphates, is not unlimited, for many of them are mined as minerals and are therefore exhaustible. The imported feeding stuffs are often cheap because they have been grown at the expense of the land—somewhere; by those same exhaustive methods which have been described and are in the end so disastrous. Fertility—or more accurately, productivity—secured and maintained in this way is not genuine fertility. It is not self-contained and obviously cannot be permanent. It is fertility imported at the expense of fertility elsewhere. It must come to an end as the mines or the land on which the feeding stuffs are grown become exhausted. Farming based on it could be described as being biologically subsidized, at the expense of other land. It can endure only as long as that other land endures. The more people practise that kind of farming the sooner must the end come. A good deal of the 'successful' farming in this country is, to a greater or less degree, of that kind. To the extent that it is so, its wider adoption would profit us nothing.

Competition with exhaustive farming abroad has led to a situation in which only under exceptional conditions can farming pay in Britain, and then chiefly when it is rather trading in fertility than farming; and so under ordinary conditions to a general deterioration of the soil and of everything dependent on the soil. British farmers are often accused of being inefficient. Even if they were really generally inefficient in a wide sense of the word, which they are not, they would have plenty of excuse. Their best efforts have been subject to the most constant discouragement. In such circumstances there can be little blame laid on any one who tries to do things as cheaply as possible and to take as little risk as possible. They have been forced to play for safety, and that means the employment of as little labour as possible, and consequently a low standard of farming. They have been forced to concentrate on marketing rather than on farming, and some farmers who happen to have an aptitude for that sort of thing have not resisted the temptation to become dealers rather than farmers.

Relatively very few people have paid much attention to this sad state of affairs, except when the threat of war has made them anxious about their food supplies, for other matters have appeared to be so much more important—or more profitable. Industry, as distinct from farming, has been our preoccupation, and industrialization has affected our mentality. Farming is ignored in the prevailing outlook on life. Industry can be organized on a big scale; it has thus gained all power and privilege and political influence.

Urban concentration has made inevitable the power and predominance of the distributive trades, with its accompaniment of a very big difference between the price paid by the consumer and that received by the producer. A distributor is in the same position as most 'industrial undertakings, in that he need not do business if he does not want to. A farmer is rarely in that advantageous position. Nature carries on independently of the price situation. So the farmer has to take what he can get and make the best of it. No wonder he cannot pay his men a wage comparable with that of an unskilled industrial worker. That is a fact which he deplores more than any one, both as a humanitarian and because his most promising men and boys are always leaving. The old friendships and team work once so characteristic of the life of a farm are fast disappearing, and the quality of the work is suffering. Work on a farm is becoming a despised occupation. Parents often object to their daughters marrying a young man so long as he remains a farm worker. So he leaves.

The source of the nation's vitality is more nearly dried up than casual consideration would suggest. For much of the apparent residual vitality which shows itself in the countryside is not inherent or real, but depends on a continual outflow of money from the towns, whose rich people want a holiday place or a hobby. More and more farm-houses are bought up as rich men's country houses; often the only nuisance from the rich man's point of view is the difficulty in disposing of the attached land at a reasonable rent. The only alternative for the rich man is to 'farm the land himself,' and conceal or joke about his losses according to his temperament. This rich man's farming is merely a form of the unending absorption of the country by the towns. Another form is that which accompanies the activities of the speculative builder, the result of whose efforts is usually neither town nor country and has rarely anything to recommend it. The speculative builder's success is, however, dependent on a genuine urge in his customers; a revolt against town life, unconscious but powerful. Unhappily it lacks understanding and constructiveness, so its result is nothing but a hideous incoherence: a new kind of desert of concrete, tarmac, and asbestos.

And so, by such processes as these and by many others it comes about that the land and all that it stands for becomes ever more and more remotely associated with the average person's life, and man is more and more unhappy. Probably nature must win in the end, even against the apparently almost all-powerful machine which is modern finance. That is poor consolation to this or the next few generations if the victory is to be long delayed and won at too heavy a cost; such cost as might be involved in, for instance, the extermination of much of the earth's population by war or pestilence. Who is bold enough to say that either or both are very unlikely events?

CHAPTER TWO

*Standards of health — evidence of ill health — hygiene and pre-
vention — doctors — plants and animals — health and farming —
comparative studies of health — experiments with animals — the
whole diet — quality and price of food — qualitative deterioration —
purity — perversion of taste — the illusion of plenty — waste — the
rule of return*

FARMING IS THE CRITICAL LINK in that unceasing flow of
material substance which is the physical aspect of man. Having
looked at farming and seen that it is sick, let us look at man and the
domestic animals and see how they are faring. If they too are sick
there must be some suspicion of relationship between the two sick-
nesses; especially if the sickness of man and his animals is otherwise
difficult to account for. But in considering man and animals we are
up against a difficulty. It is this: how are sickness or health to be
defined, or with what state, present or past, actual or hypothetical,
is any present condition which may be found to be compared? Exact
records of past states of health in any form which could be called
scientific are not available, still less in conjunction with exact
records of the biological environment accompanying them. Insofar
as we try to assess any improvement or deterioration of health over
any considerable period, we can only rely on accumulated impressions. These may carry conviction, but do not constitute scientific
proof.

However, if we waited for scientific proof of every impression
before deciding to take any consequential action we might avoid a
few mistakes, but we should also hardly ever decide to act at all. In
practice, decisions about most things that really matter have to be
taken on impressions, or on intuition, otherwise they would be far

too late. Even in the domain of science, where exact measurement is sacred and exact evidence based on it is the aim (and a very good aim though a limited one), the important advances have been made through intuition, politely called genius, and the scientific verification has come afterwards. That is to say, he is the genius who promulgates the hypothesis which proves to be the correct one.

We have to live our lives in practice, and can very rarely wait for scientific verification of our hypotheses. If we did we should all soon be dead, for complete scientific verification is hardly ever possible. New facts come to light and alter conclusions. It is a regrettable fact that a demand for scientific proof is a weapon often used to delay the development of an idea for the sake of private and very often most unscientific likes and dislikes. We really act on what we believe, and it is what we believe that matters. Proof can reinforce or weaken belief, but false or incomplete proofs can be both plausible and misleading. Many are such.

So, while scientific proof of a definite deterioration or improvement of health may be wanting, yet it may (or may not) be necessary to act in the matter with considerable promptitude. At least we can gain confidence in doing so if comparisons between contemporary states of health reinforce any conclusions we may come to. Such comparisons can be made, and, to a relatively small extent hitherto, have been made; and they can even have quite a high degree of scientific validity. Some recent investigations of that kind are described hereafter.

We in this country are certainly worried about our health: no denial of that is possible. And if it is said that this worry is hysterical, it may be urged that hysteria is a subnormal and therefore unhealthy state. We spend £275,000,000 a year on public health services alone, and the demand for more expenditure in that direction is increasing. This sum takes no account of money spent on the campaigns for national fitness nor on the care of the mentally afflicted. Nor does it include any part of the probably very much greater sum spent privately by individuals in the search for health for themselves and for those for whom they feel responsibility. It amounts to over £6 per head per year, and exceeds the total value of home agricultural production.

Sir John Orr, Dr McGonigle, and others have made surveys of the prevalence of malnutrition, and the results are sufficiently alarming. These men are pioneers, all honor to them, and have necessarily only taken into account cases showing certain limited categories of easily diagnosed clinical symptoms. If in certain areas one-quarter of the people show such clinical symptoms, how many more are 'below par'? It is suggestive that recently 4,700 people of all ages and sexes living in a large town, not a 'special area,' were examined by another investigator—and it was no mere inspection, but an investigation during which each individual was under close observation for months; of these 4,700 no more than sixteen were found who showed no sign of 'subnormal health'. This same investigator found that a condition of low vitality which he calls 'hypotonia' was in fact so much the average condition as to have become accepted as normal. An average always tends to become accepted as a normal after a time, and the true normal gets lost and forgotten. Sometimes this may not matter much, but in this case it is a vital matter, in the fullest sense of the word. Man may have forgotten what should be his normal state.

The prevalence of certain symptoms of subnormality is so obvious that mere mention of them is sufficient. Bad teeth, bad digestions, imperfect elimination, are almost universal. So are rheumatic afflictions of all kinds, together with that large class of troubles which can be grouped as colds and influenza. It is true, on the other hand, that since records have been kept the average expectation of life has increased. We have learnt a very great deal about prolonging the lives of people by the treatment of specific diseases. But length is not by any means the only criterion of the value of a life, either to the liver of that life or to his neighbors. In the prolongation of misery we are adepts.

It has also been argued that any alleged increases in the incidence of disease are apparent only, and are due to improved diagnosis. Such improved diagnosis might be expected to lead to an increase in the number and variety of known and described diseases, and it has done so, quite apart from any increase or decrease of the total incidence of disease. But why should improved diagnosis lead to an apparent increase in the total incidence of disease, unless it be only of diseases which are of purely academic interest, in that they do not seriously affect the well-being of the person affected? The fact of whether you are conscious of being unwell or well is unaffected by any one diagnostic skill. People today seem to be profoundly consc-ious of being unwell: hence their heavy demands on the services of the diagnostician.

This seems to be the opinion of some doctors at least. The local medical and panel committees of the County of Chester say, in a remarkable *Medical Testament* issued by them in 1939:

> The fall in fatality is all the more remarkable in view of the rise in sickness. Year by year doctors have been consulted by their patients more and more often, and the claims on the benefit funds of societies have tended to rise.

In the same document it is said, and it has often been said before, that we are a C3 nation. It is a fact, and we know it; not only through what is revealed in recruiting examinations.

Someone will say here that the authorities are pleased with the condition of our militiamen. There are three reasons for which they may be pleased, and it is very important to know for certain which are the operative ones if the true significance of their pleasure is to be arrived at. They may be pleased because the health of the militia-men is really better than might have been expected, or they may be pleased because the standard of health adopted as normal is so miserably low. Or they may be pleased because they have been told that they had better be pleased, otherwise certain foreigners might not be suitably impressed. It is only too likely that the last two reasons given carry great weight, and that there has been no sudden improvement in the national physique. If there has been an apparent improvement as a result of the National Fitness Campaign, it is apparent only, for exercise alone can do little more than produce an appearance of health. The desire to take exercise ought to be a consequence of health, not a consequence of a consciousness of ill health. Perhaps the chief value of the National Fitness Campaign is that it shows that we do know that we are unfit, even though we do not know why.

One section at least of the business community knows that we know that we are unfit, and that is the section which relies on advertising for its livelihood. Advertisement pays when it reflects the concern of the people. Consider, therefore, the proportion of advertising space allotted to patent medicines and cures of all kinds, processed foods recommended on grounds of health, flavorings, stimulants, and narcotics, not excluding stimulants and narcotics for the mind. To this list may be added cosmetics, the main purpose of which is to produce a spurious imitation of that bloom of health which should be normally characteristic of at least the female of the species. It is difficult to sustain any argument to the effect that people are not deeply conscious of physical unfitness in the face of facts so persistently and skillfully forced upon our notice by the advertising fraternity, who depend on such consciousness for their very evident success.

But the truly disturbing fact is yet to come. It is that we are obviously thus worried about health, as well as being (to a degree which is admittedly a matter of estimation) genuinely afflicted with indifferent health, *in spite of* the very remarkable advances made in medical science in recent years, and *in spite of* the gigantic and expensive structure erected on the strength of that advance in the name of Public Health. Bearing in mind the application to practice of a torrent of new discoveries about diseases, the like of which has never been known before, how is it that we are not the finest and most disease-free generation the world has ever known? We demand more and more remedial and preventive action, but fail to see in our very desire for such action an indication that something is badly wrong.

May it not be that research in medicine has failed to take account of the basic needs of mankind, in its search for remedies for particular diseases? That it has failed to see the wood for the trees, taking a partial view of the situation, seeing only the bits and not the whole?

If that be so, then most modern doctoring and public health organization may be said to be devoted to an attempt to patch up an unsound fabric; to the prescription of palliatives which do not touch the root of the matter; to the artificial prolongation of second- and third-rate lives. However necessary palliatives may be, in order to enable us to carry on, yet unless they are looked upon as only subsidiary to something more fundamental, they must ultimately have been pursued in vain.

It is true that the outlook of medicine is passing from the search for cure to the search for prevention—from treatment to hygiene as a first concern. That is perhaps a step in the right direction. But prevention alone is something negative. It does not represent any constructive or positive idea. It may be a shield, but never a spear. Hygiene can never be a substitute for that inward health which recks nothing of dirt and germs, yet is the sort of health which we seem to have lost. Health is something much more than an absence of specific disease; that alone is only one indication of health. Yet we have no science of health, only a science of disease. Doctors study disease, not health. They are able to speak of a disease which fits the book as a beautiful pneumonia, or a beautiful tumor. That sort of outlook permeates their training, and the very intensity of that training makes it very difficult for them to take a different kind of view. They too, like their clients, are seeking that imitation of health which can be a result of the suppression of diseases. But it seems that disease is like the Hydra: each head cut off is replaced by several others.

All this may seem unduly critical of doctors, who are members of a profession which demands and commands the highest qualities of intellect, skill, and devotion to human welfare. The need for their qualities and their work will ever be present; disease and suffering will never be eliminated. But it would be the greatest of tragedies if those qualities and that work were to be wasted, just for the lack of something more; not something more difficult or more exacting, but something different in kind. If a few more could but free themselves from 'disease-mindedness' they would be in a unique position to lead the way, because of their great knowledge, their human experience, and that fine tradition of their profession which permits of no monopoly in any idea which could be of service to mankind.

A state of low vitality in our plants and animals is no less discernible, though perhaps less easy to demonstrate, than in the case of mankind, as records are even less complete. The cost of animal diseases in 1937 was estimated to be 10 per cent of the total return secured by farmers from their animals. Liability to disease shows itself increasingly among classes of livestock bred and fed for high production, especially poultry and dairy cows. The mortality in egg-laying trials rose from 6 to 10 per cent in 1929 to 10 to 22 per cent in 1934, in spite of the fact that the greatest care and skill are lavished on the birds concerned. Dairy farming is becoming ever more trying as a business owing to mastitis, tuberculosis, and breeding difficulties. Yet never before were the animals so 'scientifically' cared for. We slaughter many thousands of animals yearly owing to tuberculosis and foot-and-mouth disease. Yet our ancestors do not seem to have had to bother about tuberculosis in animals, and within living memory foot-and-mouth disease was a slight incident in the life of most farm animals; often even welcomed by farmers as it was followed by a marked improvement in condition. Certain diseases of sheep in some of the main north-country breeding areas are beginning to turn what has been for generations a steady if not very lucrative business into a highly precarious one. Instances of this kind could be multiplied indefinitely.

In plants we find a similar state of affairs. All sorts of precautionary measures, unheard of previously, now seem necessary if satisfactory crops are to be grown. An enormous annual expenditure is involved in the multiple sprayings given to fruit, hops, potatoes, etc., in spite of which these crops are not infrequently overwhelmed or spoilt by disease. Such procedure was quite unknown to former generations, and seems to have been unnecessary. And it is quite certain that our ancestors often cultivated very intensively. It is equally certain that there exist a few people who still cultivate intensively with little trouble from disease, without recourse to specific defensive measures against disease, and without artificial manures, and without any loss of the fertility of the soil.

Just as we demand for ourselves more and more treatment and hygiene, so we do for our animals and plants. The advance made in the knowledge of the diseases of animals and plants within the last few decades is comparable with that made in human medicine and hygiene. The two cases are in all respects closely parallel. Is it likely that they are not both, in all their aspects, merely aspects of one overriding phenomenon?

To repeat: Health is more than the absence of disease. The absence of disease is only one of the signs of health; it may not even be the most important. Health is a state of balance internal and external, a unity, a wholeness, a power. It is not something physical or mental or spiritual, but must include all three aspects or it is not whole. We lack a standard. Whatever that standard may be, it is unlikely to be one susceptible of exact measurement. It is certainly not that of mere physical exuberance. Perhaps the best indication of health may be a deep satisfaction with life, accompanied by a command of self which permits of the dominance of the highest faculties.

The health of man and the health of his land are not two distinct matters which can properly be considered separately and apart. Farming is the external mechanism of human biology; it is an essential part of the process of nutrition, which constitutes man's physical life and conditions his health. So if farming were unsound it would be strange if man's physical life remained perfectly adjusted. And if his physical life is maladjusted—that is to say, out of control—the other aspects of his life must suffer. If it is true that man cannot live by bread alone, it is also true that he cannot live without bread; and if his bread is defective he cannot be expected to live well. His life is interlocked with the lives of many other creatures, so if he cannot live well neither can those creatures which live in close relationship with him. If his nutrition is wrong, so will theirs be, and vice versa. Health depends on nutrition, but nutrition, being a cyclical process, also depends on health. Supposing any creature to be supplied with all its nutritional needs in the proper form; suppose then that for some reason unspecified that creature's powers of assimilation are impaired; then everything which that creature supplies to its fellow creatures is also impaired, and their nutrition suffers. So, if at any point in the ever-moving cyclical flow which represents the nutritional interdependence of all living things a serious fault develops, a vicious circle may be set up, from the ill effects of which no creature may be exempt. The original fault will then itself tend to get worse. In their efforts to escape from such a situation and to get what they need many organisms will be compelled to adopt a way of life which is destructive of the whole scheme rather than contributory to it; which is predatory rather than symbiotic. The fact that the destruction of the whole scheme must in the end be their destruction too may not at the time be perceived at all, or if it is perceived it may not impress itself strongly enough to outweigh what appears to be the need of the moment, and so will not be sufficient to induce a more reasonable course of action. Something of that kind seems to have happened to us.

Our relation to our fellow creatures has become predatory rather than symbiotic. Some of our fellow creatures are very small and live in the soil. We have perhaps been hardest of all on them. At least the signs of our victimization of them, which are loss of fertility and erosion, are particularly obvious. But if the part which these organisms in particular play in our lives is as important as it seems to be, then we must suffer if they do. That seems to be exactly what is happening. Such an idea becomes more than a plausible hypothesis if it can be reinforced by comparisons between ourselves and peoples who do not live as we do. Fortunately such comparisons are possible.

There are still places in the world where something approaching perfect health in man can be found. And there are instances of what appears to be true symbiotic living. These instances have by no means received the study they deserve, and there is some danger that, unless such study is set on foot intensively forthwith, the conditions of the people concerned may alter so much as to make investigation more difficult and less profitable. A very few pioneers have seen the importance of investigations of this kind, notably Major-General Sir Robert McCarrison. The story of his studies of the Hunza people in north-western India has been vividly told by Dr G. T. Wrench in his book *The Wheel of Health*. The reader— the lay reader especially—must be referred to that book for the thrilling details of this investigation, and for a full estimate of its significance. Suffice it to say here that the Hunza peoples enjoyed remarkable health and vitality; that they were not aggressive; that their farming was self-contained and an example of the perfection of care, nothing whatever being wasted; that their crops were as healthy as themselves.

There are, or have been, at least three other peoples to whom we may refer as examples of symbiotic living. The perfect teeth of the

inhabitants of the island of Tristan da Cunha first attracted attention. These islanders are Europeans, few in number, and have often
been without communication with the outer world for as much as
three years on end. They must of necessity practise a self-contained
wasteless farming, for the island is inhospitable. Their general health
appears to be remarkably good.

Certain tribes of Eskimos have been found to be (or in some
cases, alas, to have been) singularly free from disease, active, and
contented. These tribes had not come into contact with what we call
civilization, and their lives were by civilized standards hard, limited,
and unhygienic. Their food was monotonous and largely of animal
origin, especially in winter.

Then there are those Chinese peasants who inhabit certain of
the highly cultivated areas of their country. They are magnificent
specimens of humanity, of splendid physique and abounding cheer-
fulness. They and their country are described in that great book by
Professor King, already mentioned, *Farmers of Forty Centuries*, a
book which no student of farming or social science can afford to
ignore.

Each according to his kind, these peoples in particular have
approached perfection, and there are doubtless others who have
done so. They may not have been endowed with the highest potentialities of the human race. That is a question of standards and is outside the present discussion. Within the limits of their potentialities
it is clear that they have attained a state of balance, of harmony with
their environment and with each other, of physical development
and endurance, of freedom from disease, and of true civilization
each according to their kind, quite unknown among peoples whose
basic rule of life is different; and in strong contrast with the state in
which, for instance, we in England now find ourselves. We may
flatter ourselves that our potentialities are higer than theirs: that is
poor consolation if we allow ourselves to degenerate in peace or to
be annihilated in war.

What is the common rule of life of these peoples? It seems to be a
nutritional rule, for no other common factor is discernible in the
lives of these very varied peoples. And it is not a rule of diet in the
ordinary sense, for between them they ate almost everything under

the sun, both cooked and raw, and in very varying proportions. The Eskimos were mainly carnivorous, the other three peoples had mixed diets varying greatly in their constituents, but with vegetable foods as the staple. It does not seem that food faddism of any kind can find support from a comparative study of the relative health and diets of these peoples, for so far as the kind of food eaten is concerned there seems to be no factor common to the four. There are, however, two common factors of a different kind.

The first is that the food was either natural (that is to say, not cultivated) or it was so cultivated as to preserve the nutrition cycle complete at all stages; the cycle which may be represented diagrammatically in this way:

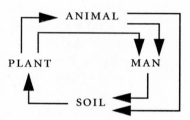

That is to say that the 'Rule of Return' was faithfully observed, so that not only was every scrap of available organic material returned to the soil, but it was returned after careful treatment by methods handed down from generation to generation: methods designed to bring it into a form in which it is at once seized upon by organisms in the soil which retain it and eventually yield it up again to plants.

The other nutritional factor common to these peoples is that so far as possible they ate the whole of each plant or animal which furnished them with food. They showed in fact a general preference for parts which we often discard, notably the internal organs of animals, and the outer skin of plants, seeds, and animals.

It seems that if either or both of these two rules—the rule of return and the rule of wholeness—are broken, a vicious circle is established. For example, the teeth may deteriorate and it may therefore become less easy to eat skins and bones; failure to do so may accentuate the deterioration of the teeth, and so on. The two rules are really the same: the rule of wholeness means no waste in the upward half of the cycle, from soil to animal or man; the rule of return means wholeness in the downward half, in which all goes back to the soil. The cyclical flow must be quantitatively and qualitatively balanced throughout.

All this is sufficiently plausible. It appeals to common sense. It fits in very well as a contrast to what we know of our own state, physical and economic. But it is not experimental evidence. However, there is experimental evidence sufficient to justify our regarding the condition of these four peoples as something worthy of study with reference to our own condition.

Sir Robert McCarrison used rats for his experiments. Some were fed on the diet of the Hunza people and of certain other tribes whose health was remarkable. They were not merely fed on the same kinds of food, but on actual Hunza food. These rats prospered exceedingly. Disease was almost unknown. At the same time and under exactly the same conditions, other rats were fed on the diet of the average poor Bengali; very soon they became diseased, not with any special disease, but innumerable diseases of every organ of the body. Another set of rats were fed on the diet of the poorer classes of England (white bread, margarine, sweet tea, boiled vegetables, tinned meats, and jams). They grew badly. They got neurasthenia and bit their attendants. After only sixteen days they began to eat each other. They also got many diseases, and in addition lassitude, loss of hair, boils, bad teeth, and crooked spines. They became terribly like us. It has also been shown that rats well fed (in the true sense) can find their way out of a suitably contrived labyrinth, while those whose diet is faulty give up in despair, and may languish helpless till they die of starvation. Such results may not be significant for us. We are not rats. But they would be less suggestive if the people whose diets were given to the rats were not now so very subject to the same kind of troubles as those which appeared in the rats. On the whole it looks as if the chief difference between rats and ourselves is that we have the greater powers of withstanding unhealthy living.

For other investigations into the diets and health of actual peoples (rare as they are) the reader is again referred to *The Wheel of*

Health in particular, and to the works named in the list at the end of this book. Suffice it to say now that the indications are that right nutrition is accompanied by a state of balance between the creature and the environment, in which not only is the higher animal dominant and so immune from attacks by its inferiors (from virus and bacteria upwards), but the higher animal achieves a balance within the species, without apparent effort keeping up its numbers while avoiding undue increase. On the other hand a wrong nutrition is accompanied by disease, low vitality, and a lack of balance with the environment, which may show itself as a rapid increase in numbers (often most inconvenient!), to be followed later by a rapid fall, accompanied by degeneracy.

The use of the word 'diet' in this connection may be misleading. It suggests that particular foods should be chosen in preference to others, and that the main problem is that of making a right choice. It is on that assumption that most of the talk about nutrition proceeds, and such talk is very prevalent today. But the principle which emerges from the comparative study of living peoples and of the experiments mentioned goes far beyond this. It may be summarized as being the principle of 'the whole diet'. Its essentials are that whatever may be the composition of the diet, its constituents must be 'whole', in the sense not only of being complete, but also of being themselves in perfect health. Their being in perfect health depends on how they are grown, and how they are grown depends on us. The soil must have a 'whole diet', just as we and our animals must.

The typical food of most of us today is white bread. It forms the basis of our diet. It is interesting to consider a loaf of white bread in the light of what has been said about food in general. The chances are that the wheat has been grown abroad, most probably under a system of continuous wheat-growing, very likely on land the fertility of which is in some degree exhausted. After a period of storage, during which it may be chemically treated against insects, it is put through a modern roller mill. These mills are most ingeniously contrived so as to separate out the skin (as bran, middlings, etc.) which contains the vitamin B and most of the minerals, and the germ which contains vitamin A and other vitamins, and the oil which is the 'life' of the wheat. The skin and germ are largely sold for feeding animals. That which remains is nearly all starch, and even that may be artificially bleached. So that, even if wheat is healthily grown, most of the life-giving and so-called protective constituents are removed, and what is perhaps even more important—the completeness or wholeness or structure of the wheat berry as a living unit is destroyed. White bread is mere filling. It is probably no exaggeration to say that it generally does not nourish at all. Further comment on the subject of bread for energy seems superfluous. Brown bread varies greatly. It may contain only a proportion of bran, or both bran and germ. But in the latter case the germ is usually cooked before being added to the flour to ensure keeping, so that when it has been baked it is twice cooked. It is well known that twice cooking has a most deleterious effect on nutritive value, especially where proteins or vitamins are concerned. Some brown breads are made of whole wheat, untreated except by grinding. The standard price applies only to white bread.

The things that really matter in food, those which make it effective as a vehicle of life and which constitute its quality in the fullest sense of the word, are seldom taken into account, either when scientists are discussing nutrition, or when the housewife is buying her food. The housewife has nothing to guide her in the right direction and much to guide her in the wrong one, even when she is not under the necessity of buying the cheapest filling food available. Anyhow, the food that ought to be obtainable is for practical purposes unobtainable by a vast majority, even at an exorbitant price. We have got into the habit of accepting price as to some extent a measure of quality. But the price which the farmer receives, or which the consumer pays, is nowadays usually a result of factors which have no relation to quality in the true sense: such as adaptability to standardization, suitability for canning, storage, transport over long distances, and generally ease of marketing or manufacture. Quality in the true sense relates only to excellence from the consumers' point of view, that is, the effect on his health or pleasure or both.

One of the most important factors in quality, except perhaps for cereals and certain limited classes of preserved foods, is absolute freshness at the time of consumption. The price of foods, together with many other criteria which determine the proportions in which foods are actually bought, bears little relation to this vital factor of freshness—vital in the true sense of the word. But much ingenuity is expended in devising means for substituting for real freshness the appearance or illusion of freshness. Such means include methods of preservation, chemical and physical, and additions of coloring matter or of substances designed to stimulate the organs of taste or of smell. Just as we aim at an imitation of health in ourselves, our animals and plants, so we aim at an imitation of health in our food. Most of our food is in fact so ill-grown and stale and unhealthy that it has lost its characteristic and stimulating savor. That state of affairs can by no means be compensated by any development of the culinary art, still less by supplementary titillators of the palate bought in bottles or tins. Such things cannot make up even for the lack of true savor in food, let alone for the lack of real nourishment.

The history of food is the history of farming, and the history of farming is the history of civilization. We are often told that there are symptoms of decadence in Western civilization. There is at least strong reason to suppose that many symptoms which are in evidence today have accompanied the periods of decline of former civilizations, such as urbanization and commercialism, with a decay of farming and the importation of food; the growth of a class distinguished purely by its wealth, with its concomitant dependent class; and the appearance of certain diseases of civilization, notably bad teeth and rheumatism (which are easily diagnosed from skeletal remains). Egypt and Rome are clear cases in point. *Latifundia perdidere Itaham*—'They have destroyed Italy by large-scale farming'—is a significant contemporary comment.

It seems that civilization springs from the land. In due course wealth increases, and the temptation to adopt a way of life based on money, and one at variance with true biological law, becomes too great. Then follows the exhaustion of the land, and the decline of the farming population, out of which the nation's vitality was raised and maintained. We realize vaguely the importance of a strong rural population as a source of vitality to a nation. But we do not seem to see precisely why this should be the case, and so of course our efforts to restore the life of the country are feeble, and misdirected.

A rural population can in fact only be strong when it lives directly out of and with the land it cultivates, and as little as may be through the medium of money. The modern farmer-employer and his labourers stand mainly in a pecuniary relation to their land and to each other. They buy most of their food, and through a town trader at that, as well as the food of their animals and plants. As, for reasons given, they tend to have less money than have townspeople, they often fare even worse. They may be, in a sense, more remote from the soil than the townspeople. The source of vitality is thus dried up, and will not be restored by any mere increase of the number of people working on the land under present conditions, for these people would find themselves nutritionally attached to the towns. Both town and country people need the right food. At present not one in a hundred of either could get it for love or money. It is not there. The commercial handler (who holds the cards) wants that which is standardized and easily stored or preserved, in quantity and at a low price. He 'educates' the public and the farmer must conform to the resultant demand, or go out of business.

Cheap food has been the plausible excuse for all this. It has been truly said that the food we have bought in this country for a hundred years past has been the dearest ever bought by any nation. It has in fact cost us our health and our vitality. It may even have cost us our empire and our nationhood.

Cheap food, cheap everything. The lowering of financial cost is our ideal, because we have come to have no idea of profit other than financial profit. Werner Sombarth has said:

> The calculation of 'profitableness' is an invention of the devil by which he fools human beings. It has destroyed a colorful world and transformed it into the gray and gloomy monotony of money valuation.

The delusion is that cheapness leads to plenty. But of what use is plenty of rubbish?

Is it surprising then that qualitative deterioration is evident all around us? Not only in food and in the material things of life, but in man himself and in the things of the spirit. Men of quality are few. A. E. Housman knew where to find them when he wrote:

> *Ploughmen and shepherds have I found*
> *And more than once, and still could find*
> *Sons of God and Kings of men*
> *In utter nobleness of mind.*

Where is that 'utter nobleness of mind' today? Hard to find, even in the country, where urban commercial standards increasingly prevail. By such standards the countryman is traditionally an object of derision, for his seeming slowness and his simplicity. His real merits pass unperceived because they are less obtrusive, and in the financial sense perhaps less 'profitable' than the flashy qualities of the 'smart Aleck' of the pavement, always thinking of and advertising his 'personality.' But (as Beachcomber wisely says):

> *Suppose St Peter at the door*
> *Finds push, and pep, and ginger all a bore.*

Quality in man is difficult to define, but it is not so difficult in the case of things; and deterioration is easier to diagnose, for we see things external to ourselves much more clearly than we see ourselves. Of all material things, that which is least external to ourselves (in more senses than one) is our food; and so it is the most important of things to us. Here, as in other matters, quality is ousted by cheapness. We seek to deceive, in the name of cheapness, all those sound instincts handed down to us by our ancestors, and designed to lead us into a right choice. And we succeed in deceiving them, employing to the utmost our chemical and mechanical ingenuity for the purpose. Instances could be multiplied indefinitely to illustrate how real quality is giving way to cheapness, especially in the sense of adaptability to modern marketing conditions and requirements, which involve handling in bulk, and persuading the public to buy that which is most easily dealt in, regardless of other considerations. Foreign 'hard' wheats are cheaper to make into bread than English wheat. Apples of bright and uniform color make better displays. So-called foods which are highly concentrated and therefore act as stimulants rather than nutrients are widely advertised, so are pure stimulants such as condiments and sauces, the manufacturers of which depend for their sales on the unhealthy cravings engendered by lifeless, over-concentrated, over-refined, and 'purified', unsatisfying foods. Milk must be pasteurized in order that it may be more safely bulked for handling by vast distributing concerns. Alternatively it is incorporated in manufactured products which the people are persuaded to regard as at least partial equivalents, though in actual nutritive value in relation to price these products seldom or never approach fresh milk, or pure milk products such as cheese, butter, junket, and cream.

There is some danger that the pasteurizing of milk may be made compulsory, on the grounds that milk is sometimes a vehicle of serious infection. It is true that it is so, and that pasteurization kills disease germs. It is true that milk must be handled in bulk to some extent for service to big towns, and that infection can thus be spread. Suppose we succeed in producing by pasteurization a germ-free milk, but that in doing so we deprive that milk of some subtle quality which confers resistance on the creature consuming it: we are back where we were before, only a little worse. Scientists who have tested the immediate effects of pasteurized milk on man and animals, young and old, will nearly all tell you that its quality is in no way impaired. Unfortunately it is the long-range effects which are so inconveniently difficult to test experimentally, yet which are so much more important. What about the children of the children brought up on pasteurized milk? Pasteurizing admittedly alters one of the phosphatic constituents of milk—indeed the alteration in question is used as one of the tests of efficient pasteurization. That constituent is closely concerned in the calcium metabolism of the body, which includes among other things the formation of bones and teeth. Who dares deprive mothers, nursing mothers, or young children of it? Shall we chance doing so in order to take one more despairing step along the discredited path of avoidance of possible infection, when we must see that each step only leads to another and usually more difficult one? Before doing so we might at least take account of the work of Dr Ehrenfried Pfeiffer, whose crystallization test for the diagnosis of states of health in living matter is becoming better known, especially in America. Applied to milk, this test reveals a marked difference between fresh milk and pasteurized milk, greatly to the disadvantage of the latter. Let us therefore beware lest we take another step along the downward path, lured by the glamor of that ill-used word, purity.

Purity is the advertiser's watchword. But in practice it has come to be almost synonymous with sterilization. Sterilization means killing, in order to remove the likelihood of unwanted change. It is the very opposite of freshness. The excellence of freshness consists in the existence of susceptibility to change. It implies liveliness. But we avoid, or are compelled or persuaded to avoid, all that is changeable and lively in favor of that which is as inert as possible. As a matter of fact it is practically certain that nothing which is chemically pure is of any use at all. Even chemically pure water is no good to drink. The subtleties which really count are all of the nature of impurities. Our efforts to remove them are fairly successful. Of course impurities in food can be noxious, or even fatal, but can be a dangerous excess of deleterious matter excluded in more ways than one; and what is a dangerous excess to an unhealthy creature can be harmless or beneficial to a healthy one. Hygiene is all very well, but it is no substitute for health. We have got into the habit of thinking that health can come from the mere avoidance of germs or dirt, while we neglect the foundations of health and so get more and more into a state in which we cannot withstand bacteria or dirt, and so we get more and more terrified of them. Yet neither ought to matter in the least, neither does matter to healthy people, and neither is in fact escapable by any one, or ever will be. As always, negative policy directed solely to the avoidance of evil is useless in the absence of constructive work for good.

Probably also, in addition to the constituents of food, its structure is important, and perhaps more than important. Not only its chemical structure, but its vital structure, which is in the nature of things not analyzable, because any process of analysis, however refined, must destroy it. Here we come back to ideas related to that of 'wholeness', which are so unscientific and so desperately important. Of such is the quality of food.

One strange consequence of the prevailing loss of any real quality in food is that a great many people, even relatively poor people, eat habitually far too much. And this is the case in spite of the fact that malnutrition is known to be almost unbelievably prevalent.

Malnutrition is rarely nowadays a quantitative phenomenon. The organism can never be satisfied with the tainted, bleached, washed out, and long dead material with which it is supplied, and being unsatisfied calls out for more. In vain does man distend his stomach with an excess of such things—what he must have is not there. In the end, power of assimilation fails, and that which could give strength becomes too strong to be taken.

An inevitable accompaniment of this state of affairs is a deterioration or perversion of taste. When this takes place a vicious circle is established which is very difficult to break. For taste is the sense on which we rely in fact for the final decision as to what is good for us or not, and when it is perverted that which is good may become unacceptable.

It is not only in food that deterioration of quality and a simultaneous deterioration in taste are evident. Most people have to put up with inferior stuff in all departments of life; it is all they can get. Much ingenuity is devoted to making it presentable and even attractive when new, and still more to selling it. But it lacks that combination of refinement and solidity, within and without, which is quality. Quality in the commercial sense is merely that which people can be persuaded to buy, or fooled into buying. We of this generation have largely forgotten what real quality means. It means individuality as much as anything else. It cannot be produced in a hurry. It is always the result of the application of human thought and care, ungrudgingly bestowed. It is never cheap.

After all, the only thing that really matters is the quality of human life. Anything which contributes to the quality of human life is true wealth. Judged by that standard, much of the vaunted wealth of today is rubbish, or if it is not by nature rubbish, it is rendered valueless by the lack of something in man that could give it value to man. Good housing, for instance, is of no use to inhabitants who have not access to the means of establishing a right relationship to life itself. We consider wealth mainly in terms of quantitative production per man, with a proviso that by some means or other a market must be found or created for that which is produced. In other words we imagine that the problem of production has been solved, and that the present problem is mainly one of distribution. That sort of idea is responsible for the outcry against the existence of 'Poverty in the midst of potential Plenty.'

The real situation is one of poverty in essentials amid plenty of non-essentials. Expressed in financial terms only, poverty has been very greatly reduced in the past few decades. The 'standard of living' has greatly improved. But what you mean by the phrase 'the standard of living' depends on what you mean by 'living'. We have plenty, actual and potential: but plenty of what? That is the real question, We have plenty of manufactured goods and more if we want them; we can have plenty of money as soon as we care to allow money to be equated to production; we have plenty—in the quantitative sense only—of food; but in the kind of food which is the absolutely indispensable basis for satisfactory living we are miserably poor, and must of necessity remain so for a very long time. We are equally poor in almost everything else that really contributes to the quality of human life. It is the greatest possible mistake to assume that all we have to do is to get the machinery going at full blast and to distribute its products by a different kind of machinery called either money or communism or the State or anything else. What we really have to do is to go right back to the very beginning and start afresh. The beginning is of course the soil. And when we have the sense to do so we shall find that doing so is intensely satisfying, and that the other things will in due course 'be added unto us,' provided that we are not again deceived into sacrificing vital quality to mere cheapness.

We seem, however, at present to be very deeply involved in trying to make a so-called economy work, of which the overriding principle is the calculation of financial profitableness. Economy is supposed to mean, among other things, avoidance of waste. Insofar as we avoid wasting money we are successful. But we waste almost everything else with a prodigality which is fantastic; especially those things which contribute to the quality of human life. We waste not only the foundations of the health of all, but also most of the human vigor, creativeness, and power that remains to us, either in war or in futile activities pursued in the name of business. Here, however, we are more concerned with the wastage of the foundation of life, which is soil fertility. The more modern the economy of a country the more rapid is that wastage. We have seen how the influence of a so-called highly developed economy can bring destruction to the soil of distant countries over which that economy extends its influence, so that their fertility is directly swept into the sea or into the air or buried under sand or silt. We have seen, too, how the fertility of the highly developed country is maintained precariously if at all by means of foods and manures imported from the distant countries. It now remains to see how that imported fertility is finally wasted. It is in fact consigned to the sea through sewers, or to the air or the subsoil through the burning or burying of so-called refuse. These are the most important sources of waste, but there are others, including the careless handling of manure, and the discarding or burning of potentially valuable organic matter by farmers and gardeners. Even food which might be good is wasted if the power to assimilate it properly fails.

Sewage can easily and profitably be converted into a valuable organic fertilizer, inoffensive and innocuous. There are various processes, mechanical and biological, and a few towns have adopted them. But the majority are much more interested in trying to patch up the consequences of the fundamental error by extending public services: public health, public assistance, and education. These are becoming so expensive that there is not money enough for them, still less for new sewage utilization schemes, even though these could be self-supporting. Municipal debt is so heavy, and demand for fresh capital expenditure on existing services so insistent, that even if town councils had the will, which they have not, action would be very difficult. As for the Ministry of Health, it is governed by its experts, each with his own little axe to grind. The job could probably be undertaken profitably if privatized, but the financing of patent medicines and cosmetics is much more attractive. So we go on wasting 740,000 tons of sludge a year per million of population, which could be converted into about 50,000 tons of concentrated organic fertilizer, worth not less than £50,000. London could produce four or five times this amount, and derive from it an income of the order of half a million a year; quite a respectable drop in the ocean even of London's gigantic expenditure.

There is still, however, a lot of work to be done in devising means for bringing sewage into the best possible condition for use on the soil. That condition must be one of biological activity of the right kind. The chemical constituents—phosphates, potash, etc.—are of relatively small value alone. Nevertheless they are important. In sewage we consign annually from the British Isles to the sea phosphatic matter equivalent to about 250,000 tons of phosphoric acid. It is an interesting fact that there seems to be only one element essential for life of which there is any serious danger of a world shortage, and that is phosphorus. We are doing our best to precipitate that shortage.

Besides the question of sewage from towns there is that of organic refuse. A few boroughs are sorting and grinding this class of material and selling it to farmers, with advantage to both, and to the land—probably. The greatest advantage could only be secured if the rubbish were carefully rid of poisons (e.g. printers' ink and certain chemicals and dyes), then suitably combined or composted with more recently living material (perhaps green crops specially grown for the purpose) or otherwise suitably activated by biological means before being applied to the land. The sorting would have to be done by the borough—the composting by the borough or the farmer. By the only valid test—ultimate effect on the soil—this seemingly elaborate process should be tremendously worthwhile; far more worthwhile than many things on which we spend more time and energy. Pulverized rubbish is sometimes combined with prepared sludge. This is a promising line of experiment, which should be combined with an experiment on the use of green crops for composting. In these matters we have made a very small and tentative beginning, and that is something.

Even in the country we permit widespread and continuous wastage of organic matter. Modern sewage disposal is extending rapidly. Rural district councils as well as urban ones advertise 'Burn your rubbish and save your rates,' hedge, clippings, road sidings, grass from roadside banks, ditch clearings, leaves, and so forth are all treated as nuisances instead of as potential fertility. Though the value of each separate bit of wastage of this kind is infinitesimal, the aggregate of all must be gigantic. To any one whose eyes are opened the contemplation of this unceasing leakage, day after day and year after year, is distressing and alarming. On the other hand the collection and skillful conversion to use and beauty of these seemingly unimportant materials is a most fascinating and satisfactory pursuit.

Responsible authorities, national and local, are important. But the ordinary individual is more so, especially if he has even a small scrap of garden. He can stop the tiny leaks, which together are more important probably even than the big ones. More than this—any little plot can become a center of renewed vitality which can act as a nucleus for the extension of influence to neighboring areas. And on the small scale the deadening influence of monetary considerations can usually be kept at bay.

Everything that has had life can have life again, and in regaining life it can draw into the sphere of life some fragment of that which has been hitherto lifeless. If you burn your old trousers, presumably made largely of wool, you are destroying potential life, committing a sort of murder. Properly composted (for the quality of the life you renew in them is of primary importance) they can give power to a living plant to seize upon hitherto non-living material in the soil and bring it into the living world. But be careful of newspapers. There are few things so contaminating as printers' ink. There is probably a moral somewhere in that fact.

Life can only win over that which is inanimate if, within the cycle of life, the rule of return is faithfully observed. If it is not observed, life lives wastefully on itself—on its own capital, so to speak, and loses power over its environment, becoming weak, unhappy, and ugly. Then nature no longer seems bountiful, as she can be when her rules are kept. All this question of observing the rule of return is no mere economic question, nor is it a purely scientific one. It is part of the wonder and beauty and poetry of living. There is poetry in the ever-recurring process of the conversion of ordure and decay into utility and beauty. If we would understand these matters we must go to the poets rather than to the scientists and economists. That is not to say that a scientist cannot be a poet as well, though it seems more difficult for an economist to be one.

There is no place for beauty in our economy, unless you count what we teach to our young people as 'commercial art'. We waste almost everything that really matters most, and fanatically conserve two things which have no intrinsic virtue, which are useful only insofar as they are subject to the laws of life and serve the needs of life. As masters, and still more as gods, they are infinitely destructive. They are mechanical energy, and money.

However, when we want to be severely practical, we still say: 'Let us get back to earth.' But we don't usually take ourselves literally enough. If we are to rise up again towards spiritual power we must first get back to earth. So we must try to revalue those activities by which we maintain contact with the earth, and which we know as farming. We have got to reconsider all our ideas about the place of the land in our lives, and therefore of all our activities which affect the land in any way, of which farming is the chief. It is not a case of enabling the farmers to serve the public better. It is a case of the public, and especially the urban public, serving the land better. Only so can the land serve them. Not until the people as individuals understand the position and act accordingly can farmers or governments do what is necessary.

CHAPTER THREE

The true status of farming — farming only incidentally an industry — conservatism of farmers — productivity and fertility competition — individualism and independence of farmers — hard work — the farm as a living whole — organic versus chemical farming — self-sufficiency and trade — trade and art — beauty and the 'spirit of place'

THE LAND IS TODAY A COMMODITY, to be bought and sold like any other, valuable in proportion to the financial profit which can be extracted from a given area. In reality, however, land is not comparable with any other factor in economics. It is indispensable to all (if only to stand on) and the amount available is limited. Thus the absolute ownership of land confers power of a unique kind. Also it is the source of Life. But our scale of values is so false that it is more valuable in terms of money for almost any purpose other than for farming.

Land has been called the 'raw material of farming.' It is nothing of the kind. No such analogy from factory processes is possible. It suggests a one-way process ending in consumption which gives a totally false idea of the true position. For if land be treated as the beginning only of the processes which constitute the total nutrition of mankind, and not at the same time as the finished end of that process, a complete half of the nutrition cycle is ignored. No part of the cycle is more important than the other, but a break anywhere destroys the unity of the process, and so impairs the vitality of every organism which has a part to play in the process. Some analogy between certain aspects of farming and the economics of manufacturing processes is doubtless permissible, for farming is incidentally a business. But it is also much more, and to push such analogies too far, or in the wrong direction, is a most dangerous thing to do. The land can only be effectively the beginning of nutrition if it is also the end of nutrition. In practice, if its position at the end as the final product to be perfected as such is that which receives first consideration, the rest will largely look after itself. For it is that end position for which we, as farmers, are most responsible.

It is a truism that the land of any country is its only source of wealth, which is at the same time limited in quantity and not inherently liable to deterioration through use or from exhaustion of supply, provided the requisite human effort is applied to it in the right way. There is thus no other asset in the same category, nor comparable as regards either its importance or the approach which should be made to problems connected with it. This is ultimately true even from the standpoint of pure commercial economics, though other points of view may be more important. The use of land for farming is more important than is its use for other pur- poses, because of our absolute dependence—not so much on the amount it produces as on the quality of the product. That quality depends on the condition of the soil. (The requisite condition happens to be favorable to quantity as well.) Quality of the product of the soil depends on the directness of man's relation to the soil, and on that relation being symbiotic, not predatory; that is, on the nutrition cycle being unbroken. Thus, farming is a part of man and man a part of farming in a sense very little understood today. It is the principal expression of every man's relation to his whole environment. Though that man be the most inveterate townee ever born, it matters more to him than anything else in his life on the physical plane, and probably on other planes as well, for they are not rigidly separable. It is the mechanism of his life, and he must make his contribution to it if he is to get life from it. He can get life in no other way.

Farming stands quite alone. Its status is unique. But it has lost its status and become one of the many industries which cater for the wants and needs of man; and by no means a favored one at that. Urban and industrial theories and values have supplanted the truer ones of the country. These true ones survive mainly as a sentimental attachment to country life and gardening. Is the romance of country life really only a poetic survival of a bygone age, not very practical because there is no money in it, or is that romance something to which we must cling and on which we must build? Is farming merely a necessary drudgery, to be mechanized so as to employ a minimum of people, to be standardized and run in ever bigger units, to be judged by cost accounting only? Or is the only alternative to national decay to make farming something real for every man and near to him in his life, and something in which personal care, and possibly even poetic fancy, counts for more than mechanical efficiency? Mechanical efficiency is all very well—it is good, but life can be sacrificed to it.

Mechanical efficiency is the ideal of materialism, but unless it is subservient to and disciplined by the spirit it can take charge and destroy the spirit. In life, though not in mechanics, the things of the spirit are more real than material things. They include religion, poetry, and all the arts. They are the mainsprings of that culture which can make life worthwhile. Farming is concerned primarily with life, so if ever in farming the material aspect conflicts with the spiritual or cultural, the latter must prevail, or that which matters most in life will be lost. As in life the things of the spirit count for more than material things, so it must be in farming, which is a part of life. Farming must be on the side of religion, poetry, and the arts rather than on the side of business, if ever the two sides conflict. In these days they do indeed conflict, and we see the results of that conflict and of the temporary victory of materialism around us today. The calculation of profitableness has brought us to the very brink of disaster; a disaster of which an obvious aspect is a risk of the death of the body, but of which the more serious aspect is a risk of the death of the soul.

Things which are true on the spiritual plane are also true on the material plane. As surely as that which is material is valueless unless it is built upon a sure spiritual foundation, so is industry valueless unless it is built upon a sound biological substructure: in other words, on a sound agriculture. (It will be noticed that the good Anglo-Saxon word 'farming' is used throughout in this book in preference to the Latin word 'agriculture'. The only justification for the use of the rather ugly word 'agriculture' might be its association with the word 'culture'. But the word 'culture' has been much abused and has come to have a slightly artificial and even sometimes a sinister significance in the mouths of high-brows and dictators respectively. There can anyhow be no possible justification for calling a farmer an agriculturist.)

Industry is a superstructure on farming. This is an obvious truism, for we could live without the one, but not without the other. But we behave as if farming were an appendage—a necessary one of course—to industry. Yet industry dominates farming, and so of course dominates the life of man, of which farming is a part, not an adjunct. Industry was made for man; yet men are now looked on as being creatures useful to industry—either as machine minders, salesmen, or, most important today, as buyers of the products of industry. This outlook prevails among many modern reformers, especially monetary reformers, whose main idea seems to be to make men more efficient purchasers, so as to relieve the machine of its present chronic constipation. Forgive the crudity. Analogy between the social organism and the human may not be altogether misleading. Periodical stimulation by injections of money may be no less habit-forming and so no less injurious in the end than periodical injections of drugs. Both have to stop some time, and it is the stopping which is painful.

In the portentous jargon of today, farming is 'the agricultural industry'. That is a correct description so far as it goes, but it is only a very partial description. Farming is an industry, but it is only incidentally an industry. The more its industrial aspect predominates over its more fundamental aspects the farther it gets from real farming, and the less effectively it serves the real needs of man. The industrial aspect predominates today, and the common needs of man and the land are inadequately served. The industrial aspect is the cost accountancy aspect, which takes account of saleability rather than true quality. The search for true quality may be expensive in terms of financial cost accountancy, but true quality is not susceptible of money valuation; it is beyond price. It is the quality of human life which is being lost; it must be recovered whatever may be the cost, and that soon. For while nobody can prove that the genetic potentialities of the human race are as yet damaged beyond repair, yet nobody can say that they will not soon become so.

The chief characteristic of real farming is that it is a way of life rather than a business, and it is inevitably the way of life of all, not only of those immediately engaged in it. It requires a completely different approach from that made to industry. It need not—in fact must not—be unbusinesslike; but business must serve and not override man's vital needs. Unless it is the chosen way of life as well as the business of those engaged in it, their hobby and their first love, it will degenerate. And this must apply to all engaged in it, not only to the farmer-employer or owner but to every worker. A right relationship to the land brings with it right human relationships. Though the former is in part lost, these human relationships survive on many farms in spite of the wage-and-profit system which prevails. There is a mutual understanding and respect and a sense of responsibility which is rare in industry. It is the natural relationship of people engaged in the same job, when they know their job and have a job worth knowing. In such living there is wisdom and contentment.

There is also wisdom and contentment in the unhurried rhythm of country life, which is mistaken by the smart townsman for slowness in the uptake. Farmers know from experience that 'the mills of God grind slowly, but they grind exceeding small.' Hence their very real conservatism, their suspicion of change, and reluctance to submit to regimentation or rationalization. This mental conservatism is wholly natural, and fundamentally sound. It proceeds from an attitude to life which is absorbed rather than consciously acquired by people who live in contact with living things. They know that the behavior of living things does not necessarily conform itself to the formulas of theorists, and that nature will not be speeded up. They know that the complexity of the problems with which they have to deal becomes fantastic if an attempt be made to arrive at a complete analysis of these problems; that the balances of the innumerable factors concerned is of infinite delicacy, and that the ultimate result of any disturbance of them can rarely be foreseen; and that for these reasons empirical knowledge is not to be despised or lightly discarded.

They know from experience that their business cannot accommodate itself to rapidly changing conditions. Changes of policy involving changes of organic balance can only be made with extreme deliberation. What has however actually happened is that at increasingly frequent intervals such changes have appeared imperative in order to cope with a change in the price situation; but no sooner has a change been put into effect than the price situation has altered again. Of recent years the government has stepped in, and by an incoherent and opportunist policy of interference, derived from town-bred thought and town-bred desires, has only made the position from day to day less certain, as most farmers will testify. But nothing can alter the facts that most crops and small livestock take a year to come to maturity: a rotation, like the growth of larger animals, occupies several years; the building up of a pedigree-herd takes many years; a fruit-tree may have a life of fifty years or more; and the building up of the heart and condition of the soil, which is the foundation of everything, can never be said to be finished. In the course of this building up a year's break of continuity cannot be made up for in a year: 'One year's seeding is seven years weeding.' The characteristics of a valuable flock or herd cannot be altered, and altered back again, to suit the vagaries of a market; even brief neglect will sacrifice them altogether.

A farmer must think ahead, not a month or a year, but at least a complete rotation, which may be from two to ten years or more; all the time balancing every factor—pasture, arable, livestock, manuring, manpower; watching growth and longing for improvement as a mother with her child. Yet not only thinking and watching, but working hard and making quick decisions all the time. Truly a man's job, and one inevitably spoilt by flurry, or by constant changes of policy.

So farmers are suspicious of change, and of interference proceeding from purely theoretical considerations. For these reasons some of them still view with suspicion and an ill-defined sense of discomfort many tendencies of today which are paraded under the name of 'scientific agriculture'. Farming cannot be treated as a mixture of chemistry and cost accountancy, nor can it be pulled into conformity with the exigencies of modern business, in which speed, cheapness, and standardizing count most. Nature will not be driven. If you try, she hits back slowly, but very hard. In terms of financial costing the result of driving may be satisfactory, for a time, but in the end they must defeat their own object by destroying the true fertility of the soil. Let us remember again that while true fertility is accompanied by productivity, productivity alone is not a measure of true fertility unless it is both independent of outside assistance in the form of manures and feeding stuffs not produced on the land concerned, and provided that it is measured qualitatively as well as quantitatively. It is by no means easy, therefore, always to distinguish true fertility from what may be called artificial productivity, yet the distinction is a vitally important one. A real farmer has a feeling for true fertility, which is health; but many modern farmers have been led or forced into acceptance of that purely commercial outlook which leads to the substitution for it of artificial or forced productivity. The adoption of this kind of commercial outlook, and the degradation of farming to the status of a manufacturing industry, bring farming into competition with industry for its share of the communal purchasing power.

In any such competition the productive activity which suffers most is likely to be one in which competing power is limited by factors over which management can have no control. However beneficial or necessary to the community such productive activity may be, it is bound to do badly in relation to others. In farming, among many other factors important in costing, one in particular is susceptible to a rigidly limited degree of managerial control, and that is the rate of growth and reproduction of plants and animals. In costing, rate of production is tremendously important, as both labour and overhead charges go on all the time. Efforts to speed up growth and reproduction can only succeed to a small extent, and such success as has been obtained is often accompanied by a serious loss of stamina in the plant or animal concerned.

Moreover, although the farmer is called upon to look years ahead into the future of his farm, at the same time accurate planning and forecasting of production is almost impossible, for obvious reasons, among which dependence on weather is the first. It is an unreliable business from the merchants' and dealers' point of view; its possible corresponding attractiveness to the speculator in commodities is anything but a consolation. Add to this seasonal variability the very great local variability as to soil and conditions, and it will be seen how relatively difficult it is to organize and standardize farming as an industry. This is rather particularly so in our islands where both seasons and soils are highly variable. Properly appreciated, however, that variability might be one of our greatest assets. A real danger today is, not that farmers may not be efficient enough, but that pressure of circumstances may finally break their resistance to influences leading to more and more centralized control, commercialization, and so-called rationalization.

Farmers have a reputation for individualism and independence. These are sound qualities, but they are not appreciated in a modern large-scale business. (But then that is a debased form of organization.) They are not incompatible with the highest forms of social organization—indeed they give it value; for they improve the quality of the smallest units, from which any such organization must grow. Nothing can grow downwards from the top. 'The master's foot fats the soil' is a true saying. The farmer must be master of his plot, however small. He then really cares personally for it, more than for what he can get out of it, which is the first condition for the building up of a sound biological unit.

Various kinds of centralization, rationalization, and standardization may be good in the manufacturing industry, or they may not. They are certainly almost always bad when applied to farming, whether that application is made by governmental authority or under any kind of oligarchical private enterprise, or by farmers themselves acting individually or in concert under financial pressure. Financial pressure appears in many different forms: as compulsion and as temptation; as mortgage interest or as offers of credit made under seemingly harmless conditions; as indebtedness to dealers and threats of the withholding of markets, or as alluring advertisements of cure-alls and infallible profit makers.

Farming demands hard work and it demands devotion, like everything which is worthwhile for its own sake, and if it is not found worthwhile for its own sake by those engaged in it, it will not be good farming. It is the greatest of crafts, and the excellence of a craft depends on the unsparingness of the work bestowed on it by the craftsman. Craftsmanship decays where machinery plays too big a part. Machinery can do more and more things, but it has no taste or judgment, nor can it exercise wisdom. Therefore no work done by machinery can be done under the immediate influence of those qualities. This fact matters less when standardized materials are being dealt with, as in a factory, than when the ever changing qualities of natural and living things are being dealt with, as on a farm. And the quality of the product of farms is vastly more important to us than the quality of the product of factories.

Mechanized farming can therefore be very unlike what farming ought to be, especially when it tempts the farmer to work on too big a scale and too quickly. This does not mean that mechanical aids should be dispensed with altogether; it does mean that mechanization can be a terrible snare. It often is so, for so far manufacturers' attention has largely been devoted to producing machinery intended to increase the scale and speed of operations, machinery which makes possible the kind of soil exploitation which has led to desert-making on a scale hitherto unparalleled, and which is forcing the application of similar methods to our own soil. Machinery for small-scale work is however improving, and may be very valuable if used with judgment, so as to reduce drudgery where to do so is possible without loss in the quality of the work. But still, the very best in farming as in all other crafts can only be produced by hand, and less than the best will not do.

It is true that physical toil can overwhelm a man if it dominates his life unduly. It can keep him in a more or less brutal or apathetic state. To the extent that it does so, release from toil is a good thing. But that does not mean that all toil is bad. Probably a certain minimum amount of it is necessary both for his health and for his mental balance and for his fullest development. Hard healthy outdoor work can be the finest recreation in the world; only when carried to excess does it become deadening, and when it has to be done without understanding, purpose, or inspiration. It is certain that in real farming there can be no escape from hard work, even laborious work. But, even apart from its great variety, it is curiously satisfying work. All of it is skilled work; much of it demands the exercise of the highest craftsmanship, and of real sympathy and understanding in dealing with living creatures. It is capable of fulfilling many of our deepest spiritual needs. But it is only so when cheapening is not the first aim. In these days to do things properly usually costs too much, and that has taken the joy out of farm labour.

Nor is the labour necessary all that of the hand and muscle alone; there must be hard thinking too. On a farm there is a best moment for everything as well as a best way to do it, a moment settled not by calendar or clock or the state of prices, but by weather and growth, ripening, and reproduction. The most constant attention and awareness are demanded, in small things as well as in great, and awareness means intense application of the mind to the farm itself, and not merely or even mainly to the market.

The best can only spring from that kind of biological complete-ness which has been called wholeness. If it is to be attained, the farm itself must have a biological completeness; it must be a living entity, it must be a unit which has within itself a balanced organic life. Every branch of the work is interlocked with all others. The cycle of conversion of vegetable products through the animal into manure and back to vegetable is of great complexity and highly sensitive, especially over long periods, to any disturbance of its proper bal-ance. The penalty for failure to maintain this balance is, in the long run, a progressive impoverishment of the soil. Real fertility can only be built up gradually under a system appropriate to the conditions on each particular farm, and by adherence to the essentials of that system, whatever they may be in each case, over long periods. Such building up of a coherent living unity is utterly incompatible with frequent changes of system and with specialization. Yet the modern farmer is continually up against the temptation to make changes in order to secure a quick return where it appears there may be a chance of a profit for a few years in some particular line and to specialize in that line. In doing so he is tempted to use up accum-ulated fertility and trust to luck for the future. It is chiefly for these reasons that mixed farming is right, for it is only on the principle of constant exchange of living material, which is the basis of such farming, that real fertility (as against forced, artificial, or imported productivity) can be built up. Mixed farming is real farming. Unduly specialized 'farming' is something else; it must depend on imported fertility, it cannot be self-sufficient nor an organic whole.

The farm must be organic in more senses than one. In order to deal with the loss of fertility, or to enable speeding up to be accomplished without incurring loss, scientists have lately come to the rescue with a great variety of 'artificial manures'. By their use remarkable immediate results can often be secured in the crops to which they are applied. But it may be that we have made the same kind of mistakes in feeding our land as we have made in feeding ourselves, and that most of our artificial manures must be regarded at best as stimulants rather than as foods, and in no case therefore as substitutes for biologically sound feeding. Artificial manures are supposed to make up for deficiencies in the soil, and for the removal of certain constituents from the soil in all that is sold off the farm. In assuming that artificial manures, especially those which are of purely chemical or inorganic origin, provide a suitable means for making up deficiencies or returning to the soil that which has been taken from it we ignore two very important considerations.

The first is that power of assimilation varies directly with health. This applies both to plants and to the soil itself. For the process whereby the subsoil is converted into topsoil may be likened to the process whereby plants replenish themselves from the topsoil. Both are assimilation processes, indeed they are parts of one process. The soil and the microorganisms in it together with the plants growing on it form an organic whole.

The power of plants to make use of the reserves of necessary elements in the soil varies directly with the state of vitality of that whole. Directly that state of vitality is impaired so-called soil deficiencies appear—usually of nitrogen, phosphorus, or potash, sometimes of boron, magnesium, or other elements. Usually those soil deficiencies are not real deficiencies; they are deficiencies of the element in question 'in available form'—as a scientific agriculturist would probably put it. But to put it so is to beg the question as to whether the power of assimilation of the plant-microorganism-soil combination is not the main factor in 'availability'. The reserves in 'non-available' form of most of the elements in an ordinary soil are very large. Nevertheless, nitrogen and phosphorus are sometimes really deficient, and doubtless other elements would become so if they were constantly removed from the soil in crops and sold off the farm without being replaced in any way. The question now is only whether they should be replaced in organic or in inorganic form.

This brings us to the second consideration which is commonly ignored. Artificials contribute to the soil only some of the elements which are removed in crops. By the proper conservation and preparation of wastes of all kinds, absolutely everything ever taken from the soil can be returned to it in due course. It is the only way in which we can be sure of returning everything. The results of doing so are known to be satisfactory. There is at least one obvious reason why this should be so, namely, the simple fact that absolutely everything is returned and not only a selection of elements, more or less chemically segregated. If we try to substitute artificial manures for strict obedience to the rule of return, we only supply certain elements instead of all, and we supply them in a form in which they are undeniably poisonous to certain kinds of life; and though the immediate reactions of plants may appear satisfactory, it is very questionable whether the long-range results are so, especially as regards the quality of the produce. It is significant that farmers and produce merchants are beginning to comment on the less good quality of produce grown with artificials, in contrast to produce grown with organic manures.

So there are two interlocking factors mainly concerned in the controversy between artificial and natural manures—that of the completeness of the return made to the soil and that of the health or power of assimilation of the plant-soil combination. Anything which tends to upset either upsets the other. That is why a fragmented or short-term outlook on this question leads nowhere, but only deeper into the mire. Let us anyhow be thankful that there is a controversy—in itself it is an indication of awareness of important differences and of a dissatisfaction with the present state of affairs which augur well for the future.

If there is any doubt as to whether artificial manures ought to be classed as poisons there can be no doubt about the classification of the ever-increasing array of sprays which are applied to crops in order to kill pests. These are frankly poisonous. Arsenic, lead, copper, tar oils, nicotine are freely used. They all get to the ground in the end, and what they do there or even before they get there nobody knows. True, plants continue to grow on the ground, but why is it that more and more spraying is necessary? What answer can there be but that diseases and pests are more and more rampant; in spite of the fact that far, far more is being done, far, far more skill is being lavished on the combating of disease by such methods than was ever dreamed of in the past. Once more, absence of disease is only one of the signs of health; the suppression of disease in the unhealthy produces no more than the imitation of health. It is liability to disease and not disease itself which indicates ill health; and liability to disease can be inferred from a fear of disease born of experience as well as from the actual incidence of disease. Ask any farmer, especially a large-scale specialist farmer, about his fear of disease and what it costs him. It is, however, not the cost that matters so much to mankind as a whole, as the fact that, although disease be suppressed, the produce may still be unhealthy; it may be ineffective as a vehicle of life to its consumer. The farmer is not to blame for that; he has got to get his living, not twenty years hence but this year; and disease is in fact rampant and there are none but disease specialists to advise him. Spraying is admittedly the quick way out, though it be but a palliative which probably ultimately adds to the evil. The situation is more than parallel to our own situation, it is the same as our own situation. We try to eliminate disease in ourselves by eliminating the parasitic organisms which accompany it, while we ignore a vastly more important question, namely, what are the foundations of constitution? Ask a scientist if he knows anything about the foundations of constitution. He will probably tell you that 'constitution' is an unscientific word, and that constitution cannot be measured nor accurately defined and so is outside the purview of science. If it is so, so much the worse for science. People other than scientists will have to get on with the job which scientists have professed to do that of serving life as it should be served. Death cannot be overcome with his own weapons, be they bullet or knife or poison, but only by the cultivation of the good in life.

In the long run, the results of attempting to substitute chemical farming for organic farming will very probably prove far more deleterious than has yet become clear. And it is perhaps worth pointing out that the artificial manure industry is very large and well organized. Its propaganda is subtle, and artificials will die hard. But we may have to relearn how to treat the land before we can manage entirely with-out them, or without poison sprays. It is also worth pointing out that the very large increase in the use of artificials which has taken place during this century has coincided with an almost equally rapid fall in real fertility. It should by now be clear that imported chemi-cals can by no means make up for a loss of biological self-sufficiency.

It may be argued, however, that biological self-sufficiency in limited areas is not important, provided that the world as a whole is biologically complete and healthy. That might be a good argument if the world were biologically complete and healthy. But it is not so. It is often argued further that self-sufficiency of any kind is bad because it limits trade, on which we are supposed to depend, or because it deprives mankind of some of the 'increment of associ-ation' which they might gain by exchange of goods. The whole basis of such arguments is false.

The suggestion that people should be more dependent on their own land savors of 'economic nationalism', and so it is in a sense; but in the right sense. Those words only imply something wrong—a lack of neighborliness—when they mean a perverse or misconceived unwillingness to trade with other nations for the mutual advantage of each by the exchange of products more easily come by in one place than in another. Such unwillingness is wholly unnatural, but it is not unknown today, when certain nations are forced into 'eco-nomic nationalism' to escape financial pressure from others who happen to have the financial whip-hand. Several such nations have shown themselves willing and even anxious to engage in real trade-by means of barter, the direct exchange of goods for goods, when the necessary money has not been forthcoming except at a price which the nation is not willing to pay. Trade as the foundation of living is nonsense; the net result is nil, just as the net result of trying to live by taking in each other's washing would be nil. It is ludicrous to cart stuff about all over the world, so that someone may make a 'profit' out of doing so, when that stuff could much better be produced where it is wanted. To suggest that it should be so produced is no crime against humanity.

There is, however, a much more fundamental aspect of the whole question of self-sufficiency. The vitality of an organization, a nation, or a world depends on the vitality of its constituent parts; and any entity which is unduly dispersed must lose the connection between its constituent parts and so become less alive. So if the smaller units which constitute a nation or a world have their separate internal relationships too loosely knit, they will become less alive as units; they will lose character and individuality. The higher the degree of biological self-sufficiency achieved by a farm, a district, or a nation, the more alive, the more vigorous, and the more creative it will be, and the more it will have to exchange with its neighbors, not the less. And the more individual any unit is the more such exchange will be refreshing to its neighbors. The livelier each of us is within himself the more he can contribute to the lives of others; real liveliness comes from within, not from without; it is the sign of that internal self-sufficiency which is vitality.

So trade is only good when it is a symptom of vitality. It can never of itself produce vitality; indeed it does not create anything. It is the craftsman who creates, and craftsmanship languishes when it becomes the servant of trade. Farming is—or should be—the greatest of all crafts. A craft does not approach perfection until it merges into art. So it is with farming, in which perfection for its own sake must be the aim, though it be approached but gradually. Perfection means beauty; beauty in art is the flowering of the urge to perfection which exists somewhere in all of us. In our feverish search for mere financial efficiency in farming we have suppressed that urge. It is no longer worthwhile to put beautiful finishings on a stack or elegant curves into a farm cart. Such things are the flowerings of true vitality; they cannot enter into the calculation of profitableness, so they have dropped out, and farming has become more and more a dying science and less and less a living art.

Every artist must be first a craftsman. Farming is the craft side of the art of living; that which we seem to have lost. With it has gone what Sir George Stapledon calls 'The Spirit of Place'; that which has made England the lovable land she is. We feebly protest at the loss of England's rural charm, and form societies for the preservation of rural England. Good luck to them and may they succeed. But they will not and cannot succeed until they get back to the beginning and realize that charm comes from vitality, and that nothing can preserve it except vitality. We do not want only the imitation of health in our country any more than in ourselves. In neither case is it enough that we should only avoid or suppress that which gives obvious pain and offence; we must create that which is good; we must replace that which is lost with something better. To attempt to replace it by encouraging an attachment to the countryside which is purely recreational and sentimental is mere futility. It is perhaps worse than that, for it wastes time and energy in turning people's thoughts towards a totally false attitude in which first things are last and last things first.

It has been characteristic of English farming in the past that it has been full of the spirit of place. Our instinctive longing for some restoration of that state, and our appreciation of the artistic aspect of country life, show themselves in much sounder form in our national love of gardening than in the formation of societies to preserve country life. In gardening many of our finest traditions are enshrined, and they survive in spite of the drag of the towns and the spread of ugliness. Our love of gardening can blossom into something far greater. Its prevalence is a source of great hope. It was a great gardener, Reginald Farrer, who wrote:

And if, amid the cataclysms of anguish that clamor round us everywhere nowadays, you declare that all this babble about beauty and flowers is a vain impertinence, then I must tell you that you err, and your perspectives are false. Mortal dooms and dynasties are brief things, but beauty is indestructible and eternal, if its tabernacle be only in a petal that is shed tomorrow. Wars and agonies are shadows only cast across the path of man; each successive one seems to be the end of all things, but man perpetually emerges and goes forward, lured always and cheered and inspired by the immortal beauty-thought that finds form in all the hopes and enjoyments of his life. *Inter arma silent flores* is no truth; on the contrary, amid the crash of doom our sanity and survival more than ever depend on the strength with which we can listen to the still small voice that towers above the cannons, and cling to the little quiet things of life, the things that come and go and yet are always there, the inextinguishable lamps of God amid the disaster that man has made of his life.

Those words were written in China in 1916. They are not less alive today than they were then. But we have not learnt much since then, for still in our economy these 'little quiet things' have no place. There is no money in them.

CHAPTER FOUR

The need for awareness — the nature of the task—forces of life against forces of death — fighting erosion — Britain favored by nature — organization and planning—governmental measures — voluntary bodies — the limits of development of British farming — could Britain be self-supporting in food? — ought Britain to be self-supporting in food? — will Britain be forced towards self-support in food? — the removal of incentives to exhaustive farming — money must not be a commodity — land must not be a commodity — labour must not be a commodity — the dominance of finance

A PATIENT WHO IS SUFFERING great discomfort and pain, which are not removed by palliative treatment, is in his most miser-able state when doctors differ as to the real nature of his complaint. When a sure diagnosis is arrived at, his misery is greatly relieved, even though that diagnosis reveals a very serious condition which can only be removed by drastic or prolonged treatment. He can then submit to that treatment with goodwill, patience, and hope. The greater part of mankind, considered collectively, appears to be in a state not unlike that of this hypothetical sick man before his sickness is diagnosed. But the analogy must not be pushed too far, for we are patient and doctor rolled into one, and it does not seem to be treatment that we need, but a new outlook on life. Never-theless, if we can find out really what is wrong with us, the worst is probably over. We shall know what to get on with, and what we need not worry too much about, and we shall once again become people with a real purpose; a real job, a hard one it may be, but one to be tackled with courage and conviction.

So the prime necessity is that we discover what is fundamental to our condition. And 'we' does not mean only the government or a few people who have power or influence, it means everyone. The first step in this discovery is the realization of the nature and extent of our trouble; the realization that its nature is biological in the very widest sense of the term, and that its extent is far greater than it is at all comfortable to think about, and that, gigantic as it is in terms of money, it can never be measured in money alone, or even reduced to cold statistics, alarming though such can be. The money loss, plus the loss in vitality, plus the risk of starvation in war, are probably together less than the price paid for the spread of a false philosophy of life; a philosophy which takes insufficient account of the true position of man in the scheme of life, and one which is primarily mechanical and financial. Most of our political and economic troubles are reflections of the biological situation. They are symptoms, not causes, so our efforts to devise measures to cope with them directly and separately are doomed to failure, for the reason that those measures lack a sound common background.

The real task is not the rebuilding of the machinery of government nor of the machinery of trade and commerce, nor of the machinery of production; it is the rebuilding of vitality. Primarily, of course, man's vitality, but true vitality is inseparable from that of almost everything else that has life on earth. Truly a herculean task; yet it is the task which above all others we have allowed to go by default, and for that very reason it becomes daily more urgent and more gigantic. The powers of death have been allowed to win a commanding position; the task of getting them out of that position is the biggest by far which has ever faced mankind, yet it is the one which above all others must be accomplished.

Need we repeat that this task must start with proper attention to the soil? Loss of fertility and the growth of deserts must be arrested. Deserts are now extending so fast that there are vast areas which probably could not be saved even if the whole powers of mankind, aided by all known devices, were forthwith applied to resisting that extension. Further extension is therefore inevitable; but it must be arrested somewhere, preferably before the point at which some degree of world-starvation becomes inescapable. That point may be very uncomfortably near. So the first job is to prevent things from getting worse. That accomplished, at some time in the dim future we can begin to think of regaining for life some part of that which has been lost.

It might be thought that our almost unlimited command over mechanical power, now so largely devoted to methods of destroying each other, could be turned to a less insane purpose and could, so to speak, do the greater part of the work for us. But even that is a delusion. The forces of death can only be overcome by the forces of life, among which are neither mechanical energy nor money. As deserts grow by encroachment on to living areas by a process of attrition at the always indefinite edges, so their growth can only be arrested by a process of encroachment or attrition working in a reverse direction. This reversal can only be accomplished by forces of life which are strong. These forces are weak wherever fertility is low: the real influence of the desert extends indefinitely beyond its actual borders; the preparation for its encroachment begins miles and hundreds or even thousands of miles away from its edge. The process of conquest for life must therefore begin not in or near the desert, but where life is still relatively strong. The conquest can be extended only from such areas, gradually and patiently into areas less alive, so that these areas in turn can become centers which are biologically complete and healthy. When they are so, and not till then, their influence can spread to less favored areas and so finally reverse the direction of the march of death. At last, in the very distant future, it may be possible to contemplate the invasion by life of the deserts themselves; not only of the deserts newly made by man, but also of those which we regard as established.

That is as much as to say that before we can begin at all we must relearn how to farm. How to turn those places which are least affected by loss of fertility into places which are biologically complete, self-contained, and healthy. Almost all cultivated or cultivable land being now on the down-grade, the first task is to reverse that trend, and to reverse it where it is easiest to do so. It is easiest in places specially favored by nature like this country, and in places where a sound tradition of farming still exists, as in many of the parts of Europe, India, China, Russia (and to a less extent the American continent), where good self-contained small-scale cultivation may still be found.

The establishment of centers from which a renewed life can radiate is the only possible way out. The problem cannot be tackled by fragmented methods applied *ad hoc* to the treatment as they arise of the more obvious symptoms of the underlying sickness. Soil erosion itself is a symptom, not an isolated phenomenon which can be treated as such. Much of the work so far carried out to combat erosion probably does not go sufficiently to the root of the matter. For instance, huge dams and works are being constructed on the Mississippi River in order to regulate the disastrous floods which have been so prevalent in recent years. These dams are most necessary, and may serve for so long as the floods do not become much worse. But the only thing that could prevent these floods becoming worse, and so prevent the Mississippi becoming a second Yellow River, is regulation of the floods at their source. That source is the whole catchment area of the river, which includes the catchment areas of the Missouri and Arkansas rivers; it amounts to over one million square miles. Over much of that area the surface soil has lost its sponginess, so that it no longer absorbs heavy rain nor releases the water gradually; surface vegetation and forests have been destroyed. The sponginess and surface cover can only return with the restoration of humus to the soil; that is, where there is enough soil, for over a large part of the Mississippi catchment area the soil has been wholly or partially removed. The restoration of these denuded areas cannot be considered, perhaps for centuries. Where, however, enough soil remains the humus content can gradually be restored by sound mixed farming and the judicious planting of trees; but while this work is going on erosion will still proceed and much land may have to be abandoned as irrecoverable, though not yet wholly denuded. It is a task for generations of concentrated effort, slow and laborious, requiring all available skill and resources. Engineering works must play their part, but a relatively small part, an adjunct to the part played by individual tillers of the soil. A combination of cooperation and individual effort, of a kind hitherto stimulated only by war, is the least that will do. And those engaged will be fighting a rear guard action for many decades, perhaps for centuries, before they can hope for any advance.

There is a crumb of comfort, which may be accepted as such,

provided that it is not used to excuse delay. It is the fact that the present population of the world could live, and live well, on an area much smaller than that which is under cultivation today. But they would have to concentrate their efforts and attention on the soil, and do without many of the externals to which we have grown accustomed. If they chose to do so they could have an inner life far more satisfactory than that which is now the lot of most of us; if they had that they might not miss the external stimuli we now seem to require to keep us going.

We in this country are very lucky. We have a well-distributed insular rainfall, and a soil of great richness and variety, which has in the main been preserved for us by an astonishing natural vigor of herbage, also of bushes and trees. A soil in fact ready for rejuvenation under conditions exceptionally favorable to the production of everything that we need most. We can, if we will, start straight in on the cultivation of health. We need not find ourselves involved, as so many other countries must, in what is nothing less than a desperate race with death; except insofar as we choose to continue to rely upon imports from those other countries. We could dispense with a large part of them in quite a few years if we chose to do so. That is not to say that we ought to set about doing so with injudicious haste. It is much more important that we should set about it in the right way, bearing in mind always those characteristics of real farming which distinguish it from exhaustive farming and from that kind of so-called farming which is mere trading in the elements of productivity.

There is only one time and place at which to start, and that is here and now, but we must not be tempted of think that economy can be effected by the adoption of the factory or commercial outlook to the exclusion of considerations which are more important. If British farming is to become once again the foundation of the life of the nation, and even a surer foundation than ever before, our present attitude not only to farming but to all our activities must undergo fundamental changes. Whether any such changes are of the right kind or not depends not only on the objective at which they aim, but also on the means adopted for bringing them about. It is only too easy to mistake symptoms for causes and in attempting to deal with the former to neglect the latter.

It is one of the consequences of the obscure and uncomprehended state of helplessness to which the individual has been reduced by prevalent conditions, that most people, when they think about putting into practice any idealistic conception, think of the problem in terms of organization. People even speak seriously of the 'organization of prosperity', as if prosperity were something reducible to formulas, and as if all would be well if only the right organization could be brought about. That is bad enough, but it becomes worse when the bringing about of the right organization is not distinguished from the imposition by some kind of authority of a sufficient degree of organization. The worship of organization has gained such strength that it has among its adherents a large number of comparatively intelligent or at least intellectual people. Its chief advocates often exhibit a conscious intellectual superiority which is evidence of nothing more than their own lack of humility. It is impossible for anyone seriously to regard organization, planning, and the like as the proper foundation for human society unless in his heart he despises the mass of mankind.

Organization and planning mean control, either by the State, or, in the minds of people who dislike State control, by 'captains of industry'. Political parties differ chiefly in the kind of control they desire to impose, those of the left advocating its exercise by the State, those of the right its exercise by anyone who can get himself into a position of sufficient influence. Unfortunately, the only people who can do so under present conditions are those who are rich enough. That is why *laissez-faire* comes in for so much criticism. Planning of some kind may have a part to play, not least where erosion is widespread; but it must be planning by consent. Planning from its very nature affects the vast majority from without, whereas health of mind and body affect a man from within. Planning alone cannot change people, it can only change machinery. Anything that can be imposed by planning alone might be better or worse than the present state of affairs, but must lack all that is essential.

Yet we continue to look to planning in one form or another as though the way out could be found by such means. In particular we continue to look to the government to arrange everything for us; that has become our habit. So far, all the government has been

able to do, completely dominated as it is by commercial and financial considerations, is to try feebly and unsuccessfully, but as in duty
bound, to keep our few remaining farmers' heads above water
financially. The result has been the merest patching, and most of it
wrongly directed at that. For farmers are probably worse off now
than for some time past, in spite of recent efforts by the government
on their behalf. Such efforts have taken various forms, all conditioned by the desire above all not to interfere with that 'business'
which we regard as the foundation of everything, and all therefore
more or less futile.

For instance, extended credit facilities either transfer an existing
burden of debt from one shoulder to another, or add directly to
that burden; already often overwhelming. Land-settlement schemes
are relatively ineffective, even with cooperative buying and selling,
because they do little to alleviate the various kinds of large-scale
economic and political pressure to which all farmers are subject.
Marketing schemes sometimes operate as palliatives, but must collapse in anything like a crisis (or they must become in effect concealed subsidies, as some are now). They depend to a considerable
extent on restriction of production to maintain prices. They tend
decidedly towards large-scale control of farming. They fail to do
precisely what is most necessary—namely, to bring the producer and
consumer closer together. On the other hand, they concentrate
influence in the hands of committees whose concern is handling
bulk, and are likely to lead ultimately to the regulation of farming to
facilitate such handling. The very name of the Land Fertility Scheme
might have been devised to delude the public into the belief that
something is really being done. In fact it is trivial and quite super-
ficial. Basic slag is a form of phosphate, the world's reserves of which
are very limited. It encourages clover on some soils. Lime renders
existing or potential fertility available, that is its main purpose;
though under certain conditions of excessive acidity, which are not
nearly so common as has been suggested, it may have a part to play
in building up fertility. There is danger that the truth of the old
saying, 'Lime and lime without manure makes both land and farmer
poor,' may be demonstrated in practice on a wide scale in the near
future under the Land Fertility Scheme. 'Manure' in that old saying

means organic manure, of course. Such are the political manoeuvres to which our farmers must submit, and with which they are persuaded to associate themselves. One of the most present dangers is that a kind of reform based on organization alone and aiming only at extracting everything possible from the soil may be imposed on us through fear of war or in some kind of economic crisis. It is simply no use trying to farm from Whitehall.[1]

There are many bodies other than governments which are concerned with farming. As an instance of the attitude of a very influential one, it is amusing to note that the International Wheat Conference was considering early in 1939 the institution of propaganda designed to encourage the production of so-called 'protective' foods. The foods called protective are roughly green vegetables, milk, and eggs; but not wheat. (Wheat could be as protective as any if we took a little trouble in growing it and then ate it all; but such is not the custom.) The objective of this proposal was to decrease the growing of wheat, so that the price of accumulated surpluses (so called) could be kept up. That is the sort of reason for which we do things nowadays. It mattered not to the conference whether the growing of green vegetables would be a good thing, it mattered not that market conditions might arise at any time which would make propaganda against 'protective' foods from the wheat merchants' point of view at least equally reasonable and desirable, it mattered not that at that very time 60,000,000 people were starving in China, for those people were starving because they had been driven from their homes and had no money, and where there is no money there is no profit. Thus are realities forced into the background by the operation of what we have been taught to call 'inexorable economic law'.

In a different category are those societies and voluntary bodies which interest themselves in farming: agricultural societies, land settlement associations, farmers' unions, and so on. These societies are most valuable, but they fail for the most part to carry their work

---

1. It is perhaps interesting that only a year later, after the start of the Second World War, the author reluctantly found himself 'farming from Whitehall' as Chairman of the War Agricultural Committee for Eastern Kent. ED.

outside the commercial framework which of necessity dominates their members' individual interests and activities. But there is hope in the struggles of a few to do so. The minds of the National Farmers' Union tend towards a fixation of farm prices. That policy has also been advocated by the Rural Reconstruction Association. It may not be far off the mark but it has grave dangers, especially when the uniqueness of the status of farming as compared with industry and of food as compared with other commodities is not generally appreciated. Not only can a price-fixing policy for farm products lead to demands of a similar nature from powerful industrial interests producing manufactured goods, and so to a sort of political price war; but also it can put farmers at the mercy of a pricing authority, which may in effect become an agricultural dictatorship—one of the worst things that could happen, however ingeniously contrived were the constitution of any such authority. Even the modified price-fixing accompanying some marketing schemes has led to a demand for a regulation of farming, in which the first step must be some kind of efficiency test for farmers. How likely is it that we should even interpret 'efficiency' rightly if it became necessary to do so?

In practice, however, all sorts of measures, governmental and other, may be necessary in order to tide over a difficult situation. It is impossible to change fundamentals quickly, nor to order. What really matters is not the exact nature of the measures, but their background, the spirit in which they are conceived, the real understanding of the situation which lies behind them. Right thinking on fundamentals will produce measures which are not inconsistent with such thinking. So we come back to the point that an understanding of the situation is the first necessity.

Now let us venture a step farther, and assume that as a nation and as individuals we want to bring our farming into its proper place in our lives, and that we understand why we want to do so, and what are the real reasons which make a great development so essential, and the kind of development it must be. We can then proceed to consider the practical limits of that development as regards both quantity and quality.

First as to quantity. Most of our land is now [1939] farmed at a very low level of productivity. Statistics need not be quoted, for it is obvious that there are extremely productive patches such as the gardens of some private houses, some market gardens, and a few farms in a state of high fertility, situated as islands within enormously greater areas of potentially equally productive soil which is not developed in the same way and may even be virtually derelict. It is very difficult to estimate the factor of multiplication which must be applied to present production in order to assess the amount that might be produced if all our land of all kinds were raised to the highest possible state of fertility, according to the intrinsic potentialities of each kind. Of course all practical difficulties in bringing the land to such a condition are for the moment ignored. The factor would certainly be a high one. It must be very much greater than two, for if Britain were to undertake to emulate Denmark and to export acre for acre as much as Denmark, she would have to export the whole of her present agricultural production, valued at about £240,000,000 a year at present prices, and at the same time to feed herself to a much greater extent than she does at present. And the soil of Denmark is less naturally fertile than ours, and her farming, though it is relatively intensive, is not up to market garden standards, still less up to those of the kitchen garden. On the other hand the factor may well be less than 51, which would be that derived from multiplying by three the figure of maximum permanent population per acre (over 17) arrived at by Professor Willcox in his book, *Nations can live at Home*—that most curious attempt at farming by mathematics—seeing that one-third person per acre represents about the number we now maintain. (Actually there is one person to about 1.3 acres in Great Britain; but we only produce 44 per cent of our food.) Japan supports three people per cultivable acre; but her feeding is meagre by our standards, and our figure of one person to three acres takes no account of uncultivable land. So it is not quite fair to take the figure of nine which would otherwise be derivable from a comparison between Japan and ourselves.

In order to be well on the safe side, five seems a not unreasonable factor to take. It is only one tenth of the figure derived from Professor Willcox's work. It means that instead of supporting 44 per cent of 45 million people, say 20 millions, as we do now, we could support 100 million people, or over twice our present population on a total production, worth, say, £200,000,000 a year at present prices, from our own soil. Even that would be less than Japan is doing now, and her people are relatively healthy and she seems to have plenty of resources to spare for foreign adventure. The upshot of all this is that the physical upper limit of farm production in this country is so remote and so far above our total present needs that it need not give us a moment's concern.

Of course the quantitative limit of production which is at present effective in practice arises from causes largely unrelated to physical reality. That limit is roughly the amount which it pays the defence-less farmer to grow after the importation *at prices below real cost of production* of an amount of food which represents as much interest on foreign loans as can be obtained, and after allowing for the profits of an unduly complex and relatively protected distributive organi-zation. The words 'real cost of production' are used above because, while not all foods are imported below financial cost of production, most of them are imported at the expense of the fertility and health of their country of origin, where so-called cheapening of production has led to loss of soil and loss of fertility. Such losses are not reckoned in financial cost. Nevertheless they represent a very real 'cost'; one which can only as to its less important part be expressed in money or paid for in money. To assume that the price at which imported foods are sold in this country represents a real cost of production and distribution is a disastrous error. That price would be very much higher if the nominal money value of the fertility destroyed in its production were added to it; but the important thing is that such money value is only nominal, in view of the fact that much of that fertility is lost beyond recall, and no amount of money could restore it. And that is not all, for loss of fertility is but the beginning of the real loss, which can only be expressed in terms of human suffering.

As regards quality, the limit of development is perfection, which is unattainable. The apparent financial cost of aiming at quality above all may seem high; yet if we succeed in looking after that, quantity will look after itself. The optimum conditions are the same for both, provided that quality in the true sense is the aim and not quality in its modern perverted sense, which is so close to mere marketability.

At any rate, we in England ought to be able to get as near perfection as anyone. We are perhaps favored above all nations, in that we have a soil and climate unequalled in the world for its combination of richness and variety. The variety is as important as the richness. That is probably why we have in the past produced the finest livestock in the world—and of all classes of 'livestock' which derive their vigor and qualities from the land, none is more important than ourselves. The answer, then, to the question as to whether Britain could be self-supporting in food is an emphatic 'yes'. There is more in the answer than the mere affirmative, for if she set about it in the right way her people could be enormously better off than they are now; for though they might not possess more money or more things, they could be better people. They can derive contentment from no other circumstance. But it would take a long time to achieve, and would involve big changes not only in the under-lying principles of our economy but also in the orientation of our thoughts and desires.

A more interesting question is whether we ought to try to be self-supporting within these islands either wholly or to a much greater degree than is the case at present. It must be assumed that the reader is convinced that vitality is of more importance than commerce, and that the pursuit of commerce can only be justified as a hoped-for result of, and not as by itself a cause of, vitality. The only valid objective in seeking any greater degree of self-support must be improvement in the basic condition of the people's lives and none other. Self-support for its own sake is as futile as trade for its own sake. It would obviously be absurd, for instance, as well as being very difficult, to set to work to replace by home produce of some kind all oranges or bananas or out-of-season fruits. Many people would miss tea and coffee and chocolate and wine, all of which are probably quite harmless if taken as delicacies and not as habits. So the right answer must be something like the following: we should aim at making this country self-supporting exactly insofar as we can produce food of better quality at home than can be imported from abroad. But we must remember that food of better quality is food which has vitality, individuality, freshness; food which is grown right, not only food which looks right; food which is effective as a vehicle of life and is not either mere stimulant or mere filling; food which will bring the people nearer to the soil from which they sprang. It is not easy to fulfill such conditions in imported food. Indeed it would almost certainly be better for humanity at large if trade in food, other than a few delicacies, were unknown; and it may be hazarded that if it were unknown, other kinds of trade and commerce would tend to flourish exceedingly.

The right kind and degree of self-support will settle itself if we can only keep the right aim in mind. That aim can only be the development of as much soil as possible to the highest possible condition of vitality. Obedience to the rule of return is the first condition of fulfillment of that aim. That rule applies to the downward half of the nutrition cycle. Simultaneously, we must proceed to apply the rule of wholeness to the upward half. There is no fear of a very sudden reduction of imports, for it will take a very long time to get going at all, and meanwhile we must continue to import staple foods as necessary, and harmless luxuries as desired. A mere increase of production in terms of quantity might not take so long; but any such increase would probably not be enduring, and our last state might be worse than the first. It is much more important that a right relationship between the soil and ourselves should be established than that we should aim at producing particular kinds of food. Nevertheless it would probably be practical to have in view at first the production of such foods as will not keep or ought not to be kept; in particular the production of fresh vegetables as near as possible to the point of consumption. But they must be produced in the right way or the benefit will be illusory. It will take a long time because such changes cannot come about except in response to a real impulse from the people, collectively and individually. Authority can do little more than support or hinder the developments arising from such impulses. The urge must come from newly awakened desires in the people; its development must wait on a change of taste. Let us hope that it may come before it is forced upon us—perhaps too late—by mere shame and disgust at, for instance, the rottenness of our teeth and our insides.

There is, however, yet another form in which the same kind of question may very pertinently be put. It is: Will Britain be forced to try within no very long period of years to be much more self-supporting in food than she is at present? That she may have to do so because of war remains only too probable but is only one side of the question. The kind of increase demanded in the event of war might involve still further exhaustion of the soil. It would not be self-support in any real sense, it would be living on capital, and we should be worse off after it than before; it would not add to our vitality but would use up our already slender reserves. Wars and rumors of wars—these are but the beginning of troubles. No, the reason may well be that soil erosion and loss of fertility are spreading too fast in many of the principal food-producing areas of the world to be arrested short of the point at which some degree of world starvation sets in. The existence of a possibility of world starvation is no wild surmise. Such an event is a very real possibility, and no very distant one at that, even though the present fall in the birth rate should persist, and even though the population of the world be decimated by war or pestilence. We may yet find ourselves in the position of having to try to produce more food for ourselves for very urgent reasons which have nothing to do with war. The best preparation for such contingencies is to adopt a right outlook in matters concerned with the soil at once, and to do so for the right reasons. The fear of disaster alone is not likely to lead us into a right outlook, though it might be a spur to greater endeavor if the direction which endeavor must take were already well established.

How can a right direction for endeavor be established? It is difficult to see how it can become so established while the present incentives to exhaustive farming are so strong. Economic or financial pressure forces exhaustive methods on farmers all over the world; the cheapening of food which results, temporary though it must be, becomes fundamental to the economic system, and a vicious downward spiral is established, in which farming loses more and more its real status in human life. Eventually every department of life is affected, and each alters in the wrong direction and adds its impetus to the general downward movement. It is questionable whether any particular department of human activity or thought can be pointed to as being the key to the position, or as being the one which must be tackled first. In fact all must be tackled, together and separately, under the inspiration of a new orientation of thoughts and desires. There are obstacles to be removed, and there is constructive work to be done.

The main incentives to exhaustive farming have been described in economic terms. The removal of these incentives which are the main obstacle to reconstruction is one of the most urgent and difficult of the tasks which lie before us. While our lives are controlled by the false values which express themselves in the present economic and monetary system, there can be little hope of real change for the better. Systems must change with values, and it is essential to consider the directions in which changes must take place.

In the economic field, money rules. That is because, while it remains a universal and indispensable means of exchange, it has at the same time become a commodity, especially since the function of monetizing the credit of the community ceased to be vested in the community. The people as a whole, represented by the government, can only get the use of money by pledging securities for the privilege of hiring it from the people to whom King William IV sold his kingly function—the least dispensable function of monarchy—that of the issue of money.

The cardinal principle of monetary reform is that money must not be a commodity. We must have real money—king's money—not the present fantastic system of private IOUs which take the place of money. Let the doubting reader carefully peruse the front of a pound or ten-shilling note, and consider carefully what each word means, and then, if he chooses, delve into the origins of the curiously un-English abbreviation of the word 'Company'; and then let him consider the omissions. Where is the king's head which appears on the coinage? Why is the Mint alone royal? The notes themselves are private IOUs. The right to use them (e.g., for paying wages, but equally for speculation) is hired out by the joint-stock banks to a class of people or firms whom the banks regard as 'credit-worthy' borrowers. Credit-worthy borrowers are people who, firstly, are rich and so can deposit valuable collateral security against a loan, and secondly, are considered likely to be able to repay the debt in the future together with the interest thereon. What they propose to do with the money does not come into the question, except insofar as it is relevant to the above considerations. The probability of the borrower being able to repay the debt is to some extent a measure of his ability to take advantage of a price situation which is sure to be temporary. That is why so few farmers are credit-worthy borrowers—they cannot adapt their business quickly enough to changing conditions; but there is plenty of money available for speculation during boom periods, when prices are moving upwards. Such speculation makes prices move more violently, for the price situation depends to some extent on how many willing borrowers are 'credit-worthy' and how many 'credit-worthy' borrowers are also willing ones. In such conditions an industrialist who works on a big scale, or can speed up when times are good and lie low when times are bad, has a commanding advantage over the farmer, who can do neither. An advantage second only to that of the speculator who trades in the relative instability of various currencies, that is to say in money, and so robs you while your purse-strings remain intact.

All forms of trading in money must be stopped. The privilege of the issue of money must be returned to the king, to be administered with the primary purpose of securing stability in the general price level. Every one would benefit by such stability, the farmer above all, and his benefit is the nation's benefit; every one except speculators in stocks, commodities, and money. For them it would be the end of the glad times. Price stability is the only thing that will enable people to take on long-range work with a view to getting out of debt. Of such work, far and away the most important is that of building up the fertility of the soil. We must have, in the eloquent words of Professor Soddy, 'a currency and not a concertina.'

Stable money conditions should tend at least to equalize the opportunities presented by business on a big scale and on a small scale, and perhaps even to overbalance them in favor of small-scale business with quality, personality, and originality as its objective rather than standardization and low financial costs of production. The value of such a reorientation can hardly be overstressed, especially from the point of view of its particular application to the place of farming in the life of the community.

There are many individual theories relating to economic and monetary reform. It is not the business of the ordinary man to decide between them. All theories are inspired by the conviction that money can and must be made to conform to the needs of man that it must be the servant of humanity and not the means of the exploitation of any class, country, or individual by any other. There is ample reason, historical and otherwise, to believe that this can be accomplished. It has been accomplished on a small scale in recent times in the island of Guernsey, in the towns of Wörgl, Schwanen-kirchen, and other towns in Austria and elsewhere. All these efforts have been defeated in the end by the overwhelming power of mone-tary interests. There are indications that it was accomplished on a grander scale at certain periods in the past; for instance by the Mogul emperors, and almost accidentally during the Renaissance period in Europe. The technique employed in these cases was not always the same. Technique may be good or bad; the trouble today is that the objective is not being aimed at.

There is much to be said for basing the value of money (whatever form that money may take) on one, or perhaps more than one, of the staple farm products of the world, such as wheat. For not only does stability in that department of life mean so much more to humanity than any other kind of stability, but also it is in that department of life that real demand is naturally steady. The real quantitative needs of the human race for food must surely be one of the most stable economic factors that can be imagined. A man cannot eat more than a certain amount, though some try to. Real demand is of course not the same as the economists' effective demand. Effective demand means willingness plus ability to buy. It does not seem unreasonable to make the effective demand for food as nearly as possible equal to the real demand by basing the supply of money on the supply of food. The Bank of England recently decided on a weekly revaluation of its gold. Why not reinstate gold as the basis of our currency, in order to comfort the nervous (chiefly foreigners) who still believe in gold, and revalue our stock weekly in accordance with the world price of wheat, instead of in accord-ance with a gold price subject to all kinds of manipulation and meaningless change? If we did so, and other nations followed our lead, prosperity or its opposite might at least follow the relatively slight variations in world harvests, instead of moving as they do now, violently in opposition to those variations. It cannot always be by chance that slumps follow a succession of big world harvests. The possibilities of a gold-wheat standard have been ably expounded by D. Ferguson in *The Present Age*, Vols. III and IV. His proposals include an internationally controlled scheme for the storage of wheat in bumper years.

If money must not be a commodity, neither must land. Money and land have two characteristics in common, in that they are each indispensable to the community and at the same time necessarily restricted as to the amount of each which is available. The fact that the reasons for both the indispensability and restriction of quantity are quite different in each case does not affect the result of that combination of characteristics. The result is that any one who can accumulate in his possession more of either than will serve to meet his own needs can use the surplus in order to acquire yet more of either. When he has enough (or too much) he can proceed to hold up the community for his own price for the use of either. The practice of doing so is the practice of usury, though the word is not commonly used in connection with land but only with money. Payment for the use of money is called interest; payment for the use of land is called rent. It may be that the *receipt* of neither interest nor rent by individuals is in the end morally justifiable. Arguments along that line are, to say the least of it, highly contentious; and it seems difficult at the moment to devise a method of allocation of the use of land or money which dispenses with rent and interest respectively. If so, the point becomes how should rent or interest be fixed and to whom should they be paid?

We must have king's money to prevent money being held up against the community's interests. For the same reasons the land must be the king's; that is to say, held by the king in trust for the people, and administered on his behalf by his government. This is the right kind of 'nationalization'. The case for the nationalization of land is as strong as the case for the nationalization of anything and everything else—except the privilege of issuing money—is weak. Actually the primary reason for the demands of the political left wing for the nationalization of industry and transport is the fact that the people have allowed to pass into private hands the only two functions which are indispensable to government, the control of land and the control of money; from which it comes about that we live in a world ruled by usury, a topsy-turvy world in which ownership is more important than thinking or doing, and nearly all thinking and doing has to be devoted to desperate efforts to catch up with ever-growing debt, from which impasse government control of industry seems to some to be a possible way out.

Many monetary reformers have seen their side of the question, and many land reformers, such as Henry George and his followers, have seen theirs. Silvio Gesell is the chief representative of those who have of recent years seen the necessity for both reforms together. His proposals are ingenious, but it is on general grounds unlikely they will prove to be final. Obviously it must take some time to find the best way of putting ideas so really revolutionary into practice. There is one thing certain: violent action is unnecessary and nobody need suffer; indeed violent action causing suffering would ultimately defeat its own ends. It is the will that matters—technique will follow.

So far as land is concerned, the important thing is that speculation in land values should become impossible; just as speculation in the 'value'—or purchasing power—of money must become impossible. Insofar as attention has been paid to speculation in land values, it has mostly been directed to the profits arising from the increase of land values in the neighborhood of towns; and rightly so, for that is where the main increase has been taking place. But when farming comes into its own, similar speculative opportunities must arise on agricultural land, because such land would tend to increase rapidly in value. What chances there would be to buy it up and hold it for a rise, if to do so were still possible! The financier would once again have his own way with the farmer, and could squeeze him to the limit. The difficulty is that, although the ownership of land can be abused, yet cultivators of the land must have security of tenure; indeed they must have the kind of feeling for the land which comes from the responsibility and privilege of ownership. Those who treat the land well must not be liable to disturbance, either of themselves or of their sons and grandsons.

This implies some kind of 'efficiency test' for farmers, for he who is letting down the land cannot be allowed to occupy it indefinitely.

The present 'efficiency test' is an automatic financial one, in which he who is really a dealer—a buyer and seller of fertility—can often beat a real farmer, who is a builder-up of fertility from within. Some efficiency test seems essential, but it must be of the right kind, which means that impairment of fertility can be the only reason for a failure to pass the test. But tests will be little needed if the economic situation is such that building up fertility pays not less well than using it up for immediate profit, so that the farmer's instinct can have fair play. Certainly in no department of life could policing be more justifiable, for there are few greater crimes against humanity than 'letting down the land'. Therefore a system of tenure must be devised which gives security both to the cultivator in his work, and to the community at large against speculation in and misuse of land.

Henry George's proposal amounts to the basing of all taxation on the site (or unoccupied) value of land. The occupier pays the tax, so it pays him best to develop the land to the utmost, so that the difference between the value of what the land produces and the amount of the tax is as great as possible. Holding the land for resale or awaiting development will be expensive under this arrangement, prohibitively so in the case of valuable land. When the bare site value of land rises the tax rises, so all so-called 'unearned increment' benefits the community and not the individual. Gesell, on the other hand, suggests the transfer of land ownership to the State, compensating the present owners by means of interest-bearing bonds, the source of that interest being the rent of the land which would of course be paid to the State. As land values increase and interest rates fall, both of which Gesell presupposes, the State benefits progressively, so that the reduction and ultimate extinction of all taxation can be envisaged. No subletting would be allowed, every occupier being a direct tenant of the State, with security of tenure subject to good use, and paying a higher rent for non-productive than for productive use.

The proposals of Gesell are nearer to 'land nationalization' in the popular sense of the word than are those of Henry George. Actually any one who says he is or is not in favor of land nationalization may mean one of half a dozen different things. Land nationalization is no panacea; in fact it might be very harmful. Its success or otherwise depends on many things: not only on the method by which it is carried out, but still more on the purpose for which it is carried out, and on the ideas which lie behind that purpose. If the main purpose is simply the transfer to the State (with a capital 'S') of the profits now arising from the ownership of land (or for that matter those arising from the control of money) the procedure will be worse than useless. It will merely substitute an inhuman and probably inefficient landlord (or banker) for one who is usually human and often efficient. The main object must be the protection of the land itself from misuse, and as a corollary the protection of the community from the effects of the misuse of land. A situation must be brought about in which every inducement will be towards the better use of land; the inducements being not necessarily only financial, and the better use being of any kind which tends towards improved fertility. It does not matter whether those conditions are produced by something which can be called land nationalization or by something else. Financial compensation of some kind is sure to be a part of any scheme. But the real compensation, for the rich man as well as for the poor, for any losses sustained from the institution of land or monetary reform will not be the financial compensation. It will be that of living in a world where first things are first, and where every man, every institution, and every country is not forced into murderous competition with every neighbor.

It is that kind of competition which has brought about a position in which the status of labour is lowered to that of a commodity, forced like others to cut its price at the expense of quality, and at the same time to hold back from the market or adopt other equally wasteful devices in order to keep up its price. In the days of slavery labour was more obviously a commodity than it is today; it is, however, questionable whether it was more really so. It need hardly be said that 'Labour' in the collective sense means people who have little or nothing but some combination of brain and muscle to live by, and it includes the most highly skilled and qualified as well as the least so—the technician and the artist and the farmer as well as the navy. The elevation of the status of labour is a matter of economics rather than of politics; of the elimination of the disastrous urge to all-round cheapening and to ever-increasing haste which involves an all-round lowering of quality. The question has, however, been attacked mainly on the political side, through the so-called Labour Movement. The ineffectiveness of this attack is shown by the divided state of that movement today; a division partly due to the fact that a few of its members have seen that something more is needed. Among those few, one of the most courageous and original thinkers is S. G. Hobson. Probably the best exposition of his views is to be found in a book which was not meant primarily as an exposition, namely in his autobiography, published under the title *Pilgrim to the Left*. He is a doer as well as a thinker, as the story of the Building Guild, told for the first time in that book, clearly shows.

Hobson sees very clearly the loss incurred in the competitive devaluation of labour inherent in our present economy; a loss arising mainly from loss of responsibility and of opportunity for initiative in the individual, a very real dehumanizing process. For that economic system, operating as it does through wages, he would substitute a sort of guild system, in which responsibility and initiative are the basis of the smallest units, from the individual upwards, the bigger units being built up from these; so that the process of the formation of a big concern, which may comprise an entire industry, is one of evolution rather than of devolution. The result should be the formation of a healthy organic whole, rather than of the kind of vast concatenation of dependencies which is typical of the organization of business today, and which so soon becomes a mere machine and often a very clumsy one too. In such a machine an increasing proportion of workers are people who merely get a job because they cannot get anything better. It is not their interest and is not their life.

How desirable it seems that wherever farming on anything but the one-man scale prevails or should prevail, its organization should be founded on some such principles. For we know that the worker on the land must live in a special and intimate relationship with the land; a kind of relationship hardly compatible with the existence of a competitive wage system, however regulated. For though Agricultural Wages Boards and the like eliminate to some extent the competitive devaluation of labour within the sphere of farming, they do nothing whatever to eliminate it as between farming and trade or industry, still less as between nations. So farm wages remain lower than any, and the industrial dole remains higher than the agricultural, and farm work is the least honorable of occupations. The substitution of something like a guild organization for that which prevails today might do much towards the recovery of the spirit of mutual responsibility characteristic of the farming of former days, when employees were virtually part of the farmer's household, and partook of the whole life of the farm, social as well as economic. Neither the social nor the economic relationship can be right if the other is not so, and neither can be right if the organization of society is founded upon finance rather than on 'function', as S. G. Hobson calls it. Finance is necessary, just as a system of land tenure is necessary. There is a certain very valuable type of brain which has the power of understanding and of dealing with finance. Such brains can perform services most essential to the smooth working of the life of the community. It should be their honored privilege so to serve. It is, however, unfortunate when the system which they administer is such that what they do is far more important than what any one else does; so that in effect they are our rulers. For finance is as much as any one man can master, its mastery leaves but little room for anything else. Nevertheless finance is a mere machine, it is a dead thing like any other machine, and for that very reason it is a frightful thing that finance should have the mastery, and that the financial brain should be the effectively dominant type. Probably we have yet to find out how best under modern conditions this dominance can give place to an honorable subservience, so that forces which are spiritual and alive may in time prevail against forces which are mechanical and dead.

CHAPTER FIVE

The future of farming—specialization—the true economy of farming—exhaustive processes—the chemist and the economist—the equalization of intake and output—the approach to the problem of conservation—diversification—the technique of conservation—diversified organic farming a practical proposition—the problem of distribution—back to the land?—town and country—decentralization—the part of governments—the farmers' responsibility—the curse of Adam—the conquest of nature

WHEN THE FORCES OF LIFE have found out how to use mechanical forces for the ends of life rather than for the ends of death, then farming will be relieved of that load which now prevents its developing along the right lines. Any such development must come naturally and must not be imposed from above or it will not be on the right lines. Bearing in mind, however, the charac-teristics of real farming as distinct from that farming which is mere trading in, or processing of, stolen fertility, we can try to see what the farming of the future might be like, particularly as far as Britain is concerned.

Farms should be much smaller than they generally are today, especially on the more fertile lands. This does not mean that they would not be very variable in size, but that the labour and thought now bestowed on any given area needs to be concentrated on a much smaller area. An obvious corollary to this is that far more people would be wanted on the land. It would take a long time for these people to develop the qualities needed, though they are probably latent in most of us, and that is one reason for which hurry might be disastrous. To get these people on to the land without increase in the number of holdings would merely be to increase the labour force on farms as at present organized and to gain nothing, but rather to lose a good deal, insofar as individual care and responsibility are desirable. The point is that those who are willing and able to exercise individual care and responsibility and originality should have the opportunity to do so on their own land. Such people are of inestimable value and importance. The extent to which such desire for independence might develop under conditions different from those of the present day cannot be estimated. Let us hope it would develop to a very great extent. Even so, there will probably always be plenty of people who like a job without too much responsibility, and that not always because they are lazy-minded; it may on the contrary be because they wish to exercise their powers in other directions, among which may be the pursuit of spiritual strength and activity. Such pursuit is entirely compatible with the performance of a steady job without too much worldly responsibility.

There is no doubt that all land, even most land regarded as poor, is worthy of the detailed attention which is associated with its being worked in comparatively small units. The characteristics of both quality and variety which are so desirable in the output are not likely to be achieved in any other way. The assumption that small holdings necessarily mean hard labour and deprivation of the advantages to be derived from the use of machinery is only justified under present economic conditions, not necessarily under others.

The difficulty, amounting almost to impossibility, of achieving success in small holdings under present conditions is very clearly shown in a report made in 1935 by A. W. Menzies-Kitchin to the Carnegie United Kingdom Trustees. Cooperation in buying and selling, in the provision of credit and insurance facilities, and in the purchase and use of machinery, all can help; but they do not change the situation fundamentally. Every inducement today is towards organization in bigger units, even in farming. That is no doubt why engineers have naturally given relatively scant attention to the evolution of really efficient machines for use on a small scale. The inducement is all the other way; towards machinery which enables cost cutting to be effected by increasing the scale of operations. Machinery adapted for use in operations carried out on a small scale may help, but machinery alone is by no means the solution of the hard-labour question in relatively small-scale farming. For the extent to which machinery can be applied with advantage to the more crucial processes of farming is very limited. If, however, machinery were applied to most industrial processes in such a way that it became man's servant rather than his master, so that man received in effect the wages of the machine, and so that increased efficiency meant increased availability of manufactured goods for all instead of being primarily a means of reducing the number of people employed per unit of output in order to undercut competitors: then most people, instead of being, as they are now, either in a frantic state of rush or totally unemployed, could have both means and leisure. The whole *tempo* of life would be altered. There could be enough and to spare of manufactured goods for all, and it would be possible to reward adequately the services of those who gave only a reasonable amount of time to the careful cultivation of the land.

Such a possibility has never occurred before in history. Its realization depends on a change in our habitual estimation of what is worthwhile and what is not. If that change takes place, we may shortly find out how to use machinery—and not least the machinery of distribution, which is finance—for our benefit rather than our destruction, so that we have time to care for the land properly.

Just as it may be advantageous to use machinery, even automatic machinery, to a very great extent for manufacture, while we must be very careful how we use it in farming; so a high degree of specialization may be advantageous for manufacture, whereas it is quite incompatible with real farming if the land is to receive that close individual attention which it needs, and if each unit is to be at one and the same time as mixed or diversified as possible and not too big. Unduly specialized farming is not compatible with the proper treatment of the soil. Carried out on a large scale, it is in part responsible for the present state of the soil of this unhappy world. In specialized farming, even when carried out on a relatively small scale, it is rarely possible to maintain fertility; for fertility depends on the balance of nutritional factors, on the completeness or wholeness of the 'diet' of the plants and animals concerned and of the soil itself. It is (once more) not the same thing as productivity.

It is only possible to farm truly economically when this balance is preserved. It is necessarily upset when only a very limited variety of plants are grown, or when only one kind of livestock is kept. There may be a partial exception to this rule in the case of cattle. True fertility can be reasonably well maintained with cattle alone; nevertheless a mixture of livestock ensures a much better use of everything that is available on the farm. For instance, sheep graze particularly well after cattle, and poultry turn harmful insects to good use; both can be kept on a cattle farm without the reduction of the head of bovine stock, and each has a characteristic and beneficial effect on herbage which is supplementary to the effect of cattle. Apart from cattle, no other class of livestock is satisfactory alone. None can graze economically alone, each produces a characteristic and to some extent unbalanced manure, and all become liable to specific parasitic diseases and weaknesses if they are the only livestock on the ground. This is true even where stocking is very light, as on some of our hill sheep-runs, where the keeping of sheep alone is becoming very difficult even at the rate of one sheep to three acres, because disease still spreads while the land deteriorates. Exactly the same is true of plants. It is impossible to use to the full the resources of the soil except with a mixture of plants (either grown together as in pasture or mixed crops or grown in succession as in a proper rotation of crops). In monoculture it is impossible to keep disease at bay for long, and in addition it is impossible to feed animals properly except on a varied mixture. Grazing animals positively need 'weeds' such as dandelion, yarrow, plantain, burnet, and all the charming variety of our native pastures. It has even been found to be worthwhile sowing them specially on reclaimed heath lands where they are not naturally present.

Here is indeed a vital principle. It is not to be understood by analytical methods of reasoning, for the result of such methods must be that something gets left out. The wholeness of nature is in question. We have tried for generations to arrive at an understanding of nature by a process of analysis, and the result is mainly a bewildering complication serving mainly to show how little our knowledge amounts to and how much there is still to learn; and leading to the devotion of many lives to the pursuit of detail in highly specialized lines with a more or less complete loss of perception of the whole picture.

So, whatever else it is, farming must be mixed farming—as mixed as possible. At least in some countries and some districts farmers cling obstinately today to mixed farming, and though they incur sometimes the criticism of economists for doing so, they are fundamentally right. For it is on the principles of mixed farming that the building up of fertility depends; on the mutual reactions and interdependence of crops and livestock, and on the entire avoidance of waste which only varied crops and varied livestock can provide for. Mixed farming is economical farming, for only by its practice can the earth be made to yield a genuine increase. Other kinds of farming are wholly or mainly trading in the elements of fertility, whether these elements be stolen from distant lands or obtained by means of honest biological exchange; which is not necessarily the same thing as a commercially honest purchase. A low price for wheat, for instance, may be commercially honest, but if it is made possible by the robbing of soil fertility, it is biologically dishonest. The penalties of biological dishonesty are more severe than those of commercial dishonesty.

The true economy of farming has been largely obscured by the obtrusiveness of a superimposed financial economy. These two aspects of farm economy need not necessarily be opposed or inconsistent one with the other, but they have in fact largely become so, since the time when machinery made the exhaustion of virgin soil so attractive a proposition financially, with the corollary that farming based on the availability of large quantities of financially cheap but biologically expensive feeding-stuffs became a more immediately attractive proposition than self-contained inherently productive farming.

During the same period progress in chemistry as well as mechanical mining and transport made available cheap artificial manures, either derived from natural deposits of materials rich in nitrogen, phosphorus, or potash; or, in the case of some nitrogenous materials, from the atmosphere by the use of power from coal or other sources of stored solar energy. All these materials are made available by processes which are ultimately exhaustive, however many new sources of material or power may be discovered. If water power be thought an exception, it should be remembered firstly that, of the three elements named and hitherto considered as desirably supplied in the form of artificials, nitrogen compounds alone can be produced by power alone; and, secondly, that the ultimate effects of the impounding of water and the conversion of its energy into electricity are not fully investigated. It is obvious that a certain length of river, between the dam and the power plant, is deprived of water, to the detriment of fish and many other creatures. Such water as does pass into this part of the river often comes from the bottom of the reservoir and is sour and lifeless. Perhaps more important still, the temperature of the valley concerned is lowered, sometimes by several degrees. This has been demonstrated, and is to be expected, as energy is being exported from the valley. So we probably have to pay in ways relatively abstruse but nonetheless real and important for any conversion of stored solar energy into mechanical, electrical, or chemical energy; even though the supply of solar energy be itself apparently free and unlimited. Compared with such considerations, the payment of interest and sinking fund on the capital cost of plant and dam are relatively ephemeral and unimportant.

The processes of using up fertility, and in general of using up natural resources of any kind, at a faster rate than that at which they are being accumulated are fundamentally the same. These processes are obviously exhaustive and cannot be pursued forever; at the present rate they cannot even be pursued for long. Soil fertility is being 'mined' very much more quickly even than coal, oil, phosphates, or potash. Farming which is founded directly or indirectly on the continuance of all or any of these exhaustive processes becomes itself a part or appendage of them, and is doomed to rapid extinction. Yet most of our farming is of this kind, the more so the nearer it approaches to certain kinds of farming often labelled as 'scientific'. In that sense 'scientific' farming implies farming regulated mainly according to the combined recommendations of the farm economist, with his calculating machines and ledgers, and the chemist, with his analyses of material which is necessarily at the time of analysis not alive.

The farm economist is not to blame. His job is to relate farming to an existing system of finance; to give so far as possible the financial implications of all the farmer does, and in particular its cost. The farmer expects the economist's assistance in adapting his farming to the current price structure. Neither can alter that price structure, and if either ignores it, he must fail dismally. But it is in the price structure that the topsy-turvydom of our economy and the falseness of our values are expressed and enshrined. Farming has had to be altered to conform to it. One of the outstanding features of the price structure is the huge margin between what the producer gets and what the consumer pays. This is the arithmetical expression of the dominance of trading and processing over production. It is thus at present inevitable that farming which is in essence more near to trading or processing than to real conservative or creative farming should often pay best in terms of money: such farming, for instance, as is represented by a highly specialized poultry farm, which is only possible because purchased feeding-stuffs are available at a financial cost so far below their biological cost that the dreadful loss involved in the gigantic over-production, maldistribution, and wastage of a valuable but unbalanced and rather intractable manure can be ignored. All monocultures fall, in one way or another, into the same category. They are incredibly wasteful. Whether they make a financial profit or loss, their biological wastefulness is not revealed in their accounts, except insofar as these accounts reflect direct loss from disease or expenditure on measures to prevent disease.

The chief item of cost which, as things are arranged at present, the economist has to take into account is labour. To the hideous degradation of being treated first as an item of cost and then perhaps as an object of philanthropy have a large majority of our fellow human beings been reduced. It is typical both of the upside-down-ness and of the utter inhumanity of our ideas that such can be the case. Till we can adopt in practice the attitude that the farm was made for labour, and not labour for the farm, there is not much hope. Some such transference of ideas must probably precede any real change for the better. If the idea is the right way round, the accounting system will soon fall into its proper place. The only situation in which today labour is an asset and not a mere inevitable item of cost is the more or less self-supporting farm run by a family. Can any other sound model for the basic organization of the work of mankind be imagined?

The chemist's job is to set forth the chemical implications of what the farmer does. The main weakness of his position as the farmer's adviser has already been indicated, namely that no chemist has ever analyzed or described in chemical terms a living creature, however humble; and there is not the slightest chance that he ever will. His method of description necessitates fragmentation, which is incompatible with the continuance of life. The farmer is obviously only really interested in the state of living. Farmers may be helped in due time by biology, that baby science, if it can get out of the method of examination by fragmentation hitherto characteristic of science as we know it.

The chemical attitude to farming has been scornfully referred to as the 'NPK mentality', because advice to farmers on feeding crops has been mainly based on the experiments at Rothamsted and elsewhere, which have been taken to indicate that the best (or most 'economical') way of feeding plants growing in soil is to supply to them nitrogen (N), phosphorus (P), and potash (K) in the form of suitable chemical compounds, with or without other manures. It is certainly one way of supplying three elements which play a critical part in plant growth, and are often apparently deficient.

In parenthesis, the reader may be reminded that the favorable effects of chemical treatment on plants as regards their health and quality has recently been seriously and increasingly called in question. It seems that they are like many, or most, drugs or remedies, in that the more you use the more you have to use, and that reliance on them is accompanied by the appearance of seemingly new deficiencies or diseases, which in turn have to be made up or remedied. Fifteen to twenty times the amount of copper salts per acre seems now to be necessary to keep down phylloxera on vines, as compared with a few decades ago. Boron and manganese represent deficiencies recently detected in certain unhealthy plants, while for animals the list is now much longer, and includes (besides phosphorus, iron, and calcium) manganese, zinc, aluminum, copper, molybdenum, and cobalt. To grow a bushel of wheat, we now apply about three times the amount of nitrogen commonly applied in the past.

This aspect of affairs has been more fully discussed elsewhere. It is of course intimately related to economics, but the main point here is that reliance on deposited or accumulated material or energy for maintenance purposes is of necessity exhaustive. In the language of finance, it is living on capital. Life is then taking more than it is giving. Clearly then, if life in its present presumably fairly highly evolved form is to persist at all, if destruction, slow or fast, is not to overtake at least the higher forms of life (the fact that in a few million years they might be again evolved out of surviving forms can be only a poor consolation), then the output or expenditure of life as a whole must at least be equalled by its intake or gain. How ar we to know whether that is the case or not? By one simple and straightforward test: by inquiring as to whether the rate of formation of fertile soil exceeds, equals, or is exceeded by the rate of destruction of fertile soil, taking the world as a whole. The answer as it affects the present time is painfully easy to arrive at—and has already been given.

The fundamental economics of farming can only be expressed in terms of total effect on the fertility of the world. The relatively specialized farmer of today, with his complex requirements for his farm and himself, can with difficulty, if at all, escape from the predominance of the financial aspect of all that he does. It certainly does not pay him to impair the productivity of his farm—he who does so is and always has been a bad farmer. But the successful farmer of today is usually one who is successful in maintaining the productivity of his soil by the purchase of materials—feeding-stuffs or manures—which are cheap because they are produced at the expense of fertility elsewhere. But that kind of successful farmer may not be a better farmer than another less 'successful'; he may be only a more successful business man.

Therefore either the financial and economic complex in which we live must be so altered that the direction of the pressure which it exercises is changed, or alternatively at least some farmers or communities must insulate themselves from it. It may be that the alterations required in the economic complex can only be brought about by the building up from its biological elements of a new kind of community which is biologically self-supporting. And it is worth pointing out again that in the case of a completely self-contained farm or community, one which supplies all its own needs for men, animals, crops, and soil, any surplus that can be disposed of is clear gain to that community, however small the amount and however low the price. Only such a farm or community can be independent of money. But, more important, the said surplus represents not only a gain to the producers of it, but also to the world at large. It is a true profit; measurable no doubt in terms of money, but not primarily financial. The making of a financial profit conveys no information one way or the other as to whether the process by which it was made was exhaustive or the reverse. Yet it is that information which is important. It will of course be argued that by the use of imported chemicals and feeding-stuffs production per acre has been increased. That is true, but what has been the cost?

It will be further argued that it is impossible to maintain production at a level sufficient to maintain the inhabitants of populous countries if such importations are dispensed with. How can a farm be self-supporting when produce is constantly being taken off it, containing elements (especially N, P, and K) which must be replaced? The answer is that of course they must be replaced; the real question at issue is: 'How?'

We have seen that soil has been and is being maintained in wonderful condition by certain peoples, without apparent loss of fertility through the centuries. Obviously, no biological unit, however small or great, need necessarily suffer any loss of its elementary constituents, as matter is indestructible; provided only that, after passing through the phase of being part of an animal or plant, they all be returned to the soil in such a way that plants can recover them from the soil.

In that proviso we have the key to the search for the true biological economics of farming. The problem is not one of finance nor of the supply of elements. There must necessarily exist enough elements in soil, plants, and animals to maintain life at its present standards on any area, however big or small. The problem is that of keeping them in circulation, of preventing them from reverting to forms in which they are inaccessible to life. It is not sufficient to obey the rule of return in its quantitative implications only. To do so is to exhibit NPK mentality, or, to give it another name, the 'deficiency complex'.

Loss of elements to life takes place through erosion in its various forms, and through leaching by rain into the subsoil where what may be called 'mineralization' takes place. Both can be prevented (or minimized) in one way, and in one way alone, and that is by seeing that they arrive in assimilable form on to a soil capable of assimilating them. That is the only possible foundation for a truly economical farming, and a truly economical farming is the only possible foundation for the continuance—let alone the development—of human life.

Mere conservation, however, even if it attains technical perfection, does not allow for development. Fortunately there is a very considerable margin to play with. Perhaps the most significant revelation of the whole of the Rothamsted experiments is that the classic plot on the Broadbalk wheat field, cropped continuously with wheat for eighty-seven years without return in the form of manure of any kind, has settled down to a steady yield of about twelve bushels per acre each year. This is only one third of a moderate crop, but it seems to be produced out of nothing. So we can apparently under ordinary conditions afford some loss of elements, and still at least maintain yields. We are given grace to the extent of one-third of a crop. But we cannot afford a 50 per cent loss, which is the loss regarded as normal in the process of transforming fresh farmyard manure into a crop fit for harvesting. If we incur a 30 per cent loss it seems that we have a chance of keeping level. If we can improve on that, we can start to build up fertility and to produce a real profit. Under no other conditions can a real profit be obtained.

No farm economics can therefore be of ultimate value unless its first interest is that of reducing this organic loss to a minimum. It is a dual problem, at least; its main aspects being the treatment of organic manure in all its forms, including composts made of vegetable 'wastes', and the treatment of the soil itself, including cultivation and cropping. No other kind of farm economics has any reality beyond the immediate present. The farmer is of course living in the immediate present, and so is the advisory economist, and both very naturally want to go on living as comfortably and prosperously as may be. And times are very uncertain, so anything which seems for the time to be likely to produce an immediate financial profit, or to reduce a financial loss, almost necessarily receives first consideration, whether it be in conformity with the first principles of true economy or otherwise.

Thus it is that the subtle technical problems involved in the conservation of organic matter and of the vitality of the soil have received scant attention. 'Vitality' is a very unscientific term; the fact that there is no scientific term available for the very real and important thing involved is proof of that lack of attention. Most practising farmers and gardeners will know what is meant by it. It has been left to 'amateurs' to pursue those problems. Perhaps that is a good thing in the end, and anyhow pioneers are always amateurs. Allusion has been made to the works of some of them, but perhaps the names and works of many of the most important of them will never be recorded in print. They are those who will do the job and make a success of it. They will be the real farm economists.

Specialization has made possible the attainment of that mechanical efficiency which produces the illusion of 'potential plenty'. It is the curse of the age, not only in its economic or social repercussions but in its effect on the minds of its victims, in that it more or less effectively denies to them the possibility of a full experience of life, and so of attaining a comprehensive outlook. The universal accessibility (and indeed obtrusiveness) of mere information conveyed in print by no means compensates for what actually does or does not happen to a man in his life. His reaction to information is in fact conditioned entirely by his inner personal experience. The richness or otherwise of that experience is in turn largely conditioned by the mental state. A specialized mind is only capable of limited experience. On the other hand, an open or unspecialized mind can gather rich experience even from an environment which is very restricted in the purely geographical sense. The physical boundaries of the environment need not limit its internal richness and diversification.

Specialization in the modern sense is the division of labour carried to a more or less extreme point. Division of labour is the source of that material advantage which we call the 'increment of association'. But division of labour is only good when it is not carried so far as to react adversely on the minds of the individuals who are supposed to benefit materially from it, so as to deny them a whole life. So we must not be carried away by the possibilities of developing the 'increment of association' through specialization, to the extent that the quality of our mental life is impaired, nor to the extent that the quality of our physical life, carried on as it is through farming, is also impaired. Even the immediate advantages supposed to be associated with most kinds of specialization in farming are mainly illusory. Though it be true that certain soils in an unimproved state may be best suited to limited categories of crops or treatment, it is also true that good cultivation equalizes soils. And it is true that the variety of systems of farming which are in the full sense mixed farming is infinite. There is ample room for adaptation to local conditions without abandoning the principle, which is that of working towards the greatest possible diversification so as to produce as complete an organic whole as possible.

That diversification is incomplete without the presence on a farm of such seeming superfluities as trees, bushes, hedges, and hedgerow weeds—or wildflowers as you may call them if your temperament is romantic. All these have their qualitative importance and value, both individually and collectively. Good cultivation is always beautiful, but most of us have a taste for wildness as well. It is pleasant that the best cultivation of all should be that which is not without its touch of wildness, so that it should present that picture of wildness and intimacy in association which is the most attractive picture of all; and which is, above all, the picture of England.

Only a variety, as wide as is possible consistently with reasonable ease of management, in the classes of crops and of livestock kept on the farm can ensure, at one and the same time, the fullest use of everything that grows on the farm and the accumulation of real fertility in the soil. For fertility is not a static phenomenon, it is a living process of change and exchange. It is the only sound defence against disease, for disease is only a symptom of a state of unbalance. Incidentally the conditions of small-scale mixed farming are such as to reduce to the lowest point the likelihood of the spread of infectious epidemic sickness, should it arise locally. The possibility of its doing so cannot ever be eliminated, for perfection is unattainable. It will, in fact, take a long time even to reduce appreciably the need for purely protective measures against disease.

As the farm itself, though small, must be internally diversified, so must the larger unit: the valley, the district, the county, the country. A sensitive adaptation of individual farms to the small variation in soil, aspect, moisture, and so on will in part ensure this wider diversification. Doubtless, however, in addition, some higher authority must see to it that woods are not injudiciously destroyed, that shelter is planted, or that other major works for the benefit of a big area are undertaken where necessary. Insofar as that authority derives its functions directly from the people working the land to be benefited, it will work well. Only common consent and the greatest possible degree of decentralization can do all that is necessary, and at the same time preserve the 'Spirit of Place', without which character, individuality, and liveliness will be lost.

The adoption of true mixed farming is the first step towards the perfection of the individual farm, and after it of the countryside in all its aspects, as a healthy organic whole yielding a true profit rather than only a financial profit. The next step is the proper conservation, preparation, and return to the soil of all organic matter severed from the soil. Much of this is destined for consumption by men or animals. As to how that consumed by men can in practice be returned, without abandoning elementary hygienic principles, something has already been said. It is very unlikely that either the best method of preparation or the best way of using such material has yet been evolved. We feel an instinctive repugnance to its use for the growing of crops intended directly for human consumption. That repugnance may be mere prejudice, but it may also be soundly based, quite apart from any questions of the conveyance of infection. So we may just as well give way to it and use organic material prepared from sewage on pasture or on other crops intended for consumption by animals. If we look after our animal manure and vegetable wastes properly there need be no lack of organic feeding for the soil on which corn, vegetables, and fruit are grown for human consumption.

Gardeners know well that there is no substitute for organic manure if produce satisfactory as regards health and quality is to be grown. Some farmers have forgotten this, in face of the expense of handling organic manures and the remarkable quantitative result attainable by the substitution of chemical fertilizers for organic manures. But the complaint that dung is too expensive to handle seems already to be giving way to the complaint that enough dung cannot be got. There are several ways out of this difficulty. We can learn how to make the dung we have got go farther, by learning—or may it be to some extent relearning—how to bring it into a proper state of biological activity. Or we can find out methods of preparing organic matter other than dung so that it can satisfy the needs of the soil. Best of all, we can do both; and then, whether the supply of dung is adequate or not, we shall be better off than we could be otherwise.

Various methods of composting or preparation of farmyard manure and miscellaneous organic matter have come into prominence lately. Their widespread adoption obviously threatens the sales of commercially prepared fertilizers, organic or inorganic. Many attempts have been and are being made to discredit such methods, or alternatively to persuade people that compost is best prepared with the help of chemicals. In fact, some of the purely organic methods have proved very successful, particularly as regards the quality of the produce grown by them and its resistance to disease, and it has become clear that chemicals can economically be dispensed with, apart from the question as to whether they are or are not actually harmful. The best processes of organic fermentation are purely biological and are qualitatively changed, if not actually impeded, by the substitution of a chemical breakdown for a biological one. Apart from chemical processes, those best known in this country are the 'Indore' process, developed from ancient Indian practices and introduced into this country by Sir Albert Howard, and the 'biodynamic' method, evolved in accordance with the recommendations of the late Dr Rudolf Steiner. The latter method has been highly developed in the course of some fifteen years' work on the Continent, and its effectiveness may be said to be proved, though its supporters would be the last to claim that there is no more to be learned about it.

The fact remains that in any ordinary garden and on any reasonably well-balanced mixed farm, a quantity of organic manure can be produced amply sufficient to supply the needs of the soil. The ultimate benefit to soil, crops, and stock is not calculable, because non-measurable factors of a purely qualitative kind are involved such as health, palatability, and others more subtle; but the farmer or gardener can be confident that even from the start the extra labour involved will be at least balanced by the saving in purchased fertilizers. As always in farming, a change of method must not be adopted in a hurry, and the full benefits cannot be realized for a long time. But we have now sufficient experience to be able to say that a self-contained organic farm is no mere theoretical dream, practicable only for the 'gentleman farmer' who farms for fun and can afford to lose money, but is an economical proposition for any farmer whose farm is not grossly overweighted in any particular direction.

So we can revitalize much of our land whenever we choose to, and without spending money. Needless to say, it must be done by farmers because they want to. They will not learn how to do it by reading advertisements or articles in the press. But they will soon find out about it when a few have made a good start. They are rightly suspicious of theoretical talk. It is urgent that they shall be given opportunities to see what can be done in practice.

This advocacy of small self-contained farms, relatively independent of outside purchases, seems to be very contrary to modern tendencies in the world of trade and commerce, with its ever-increasing specialization and centralization, reflected in the modern industrial town. It is indeed here categorically stated that those tendencies, whatever be their merits or demerits for manufacturing industry and trade, are, as they affect farming, diametrically opposed to the satisfaction of the essential biological needs of mankind, which are of course identical with those of the soil on which he lives and of all the other creatures of that soil.

But if we put these first things first, shall we really have to sacrifice anything worthwhile? A little leisure perhaps, which we today do not seem to know what to do with anyhow. Provided that growth in the right direction is spontaneous and not forced, which it can only be if it proceeds from the desire of the people concerned, there need be no dislocation, but only adaptation. It is a kind of dislocation from which we are suffering now; the changeover should rather take the form of a reallocation on a sounder basis. For instance, the whole 'problem of distribution' as we know it is merely a result of dislocation, in the full derivative sense of the word. It is the maldistribution of production and of population which makes the distribution of goods so complicated, and which puts the country at the mercy of the distributor, especially when perishable goods are concerned. But even now much could be done, given a change of desires in the people. For example, a real demand for more fresh vegetables would soon bring market gardeners to a neighborhood. So long as people go on being fooled by advertisement (blatant or concealed) of processed foods, so long will they and the farmers be at the mercy of vast distributing concerns, whose every interest seems to be opposed to the people's real nutritional necessities. How can it be otherwise in a world of specialization and urbanization? Effective distribution seems to necessitate sterilization, which means killing, for failure to sterilize may mean infection in bulk. Hence the outcry for the pasteurizing of milk. But sterilization reduces the resistance to infection and the power of assimilation of the consumer of that which is sterilized. So yet more sterilizing seems to be necessary. A vicious circle again, of a type which should by now be familiar.

What more outrageous instance can be given of the lengths to which absurdity has gone in the relationship between production, manufacture, and distribution, than the enormous sales of 'cream-making' machines during the past few years? Of course these sales take place because the process pays. But how fantastic is the sense in which the word 'pay' is used in this connection! Cows are fed and milked in the antipodes. The milk is made into cream, and the cream into butter, which is carefully and expensively sterilized and packed, and conveyed 12,000 miles or more. It is then mixed with a little milk and put through the machine, and emerges at best as an indifferent imitation of cream. Yet magnificent dairying land in this country lies derelict, the New Zealand farmer has not wherewith to pay his mortgage interest, and the British housewife has to put up with another substitute for the real thing. Whom then does it 'pay'? Perhaps those who do the transport; but if so, only at the expense, incalculably great in proportion, of the advantages which a sane system of distribution would confer upon them individually and collectively. The only people whom it pays are a few financiers. Even they must lose in the end, for a state of affairs so inept carries within itself the seeds of its own destruction, and cannot endure.

There can be no real solution of the problem of distribution other than a rebuilding of society on a sound organic basis, which must involve a better distribution of the population, both within most countries and in the world as a whole. To attempt to look at the problem of distribution in isolation is to be led into the snare of 'planned economy' equally a snare whether the planning be done by the State, or by private interests holding quasi-monopolistic powers. The only possible foundation for a sound organic life within any community is a close association of the people with the land.

The simplest and most direct way in which a closer association of the people with the land could come about is that as many people as possible should be living on the land, for at least some part of their lives. Farming as an occupation should be at least part of the normal way of life for a considerable proportion of the people of Britain, unless all that has been said about it hitherto is pure fancy. What that proportion should be is a matter for speculation at present, and can never be settled except by experience. It is essential that the people fortunate enough to be so placed should be able to make a living at least as easily as people otherwise occupied, and that they should be able to do so under conditions of the greatest possible individual, economic, political, and social freedom. Such conditions are not impossible of attainment, and will probably come about of themselves if the main obstacles to the evolution of a free and natural economy are removed, and if circumstances force upon people a clearer realization of where their true interests lie. It is doubtful if any one ever really learns otherwise than by force of circumstances. It looks as if circumstances were changing in a way that may impress the truth on people very forcibly.

To suggest that a big 'back to the land' movement must come about in the future is not the same as to say that it can come about under present economic conditions. Much of what has been said about the potential beneficial effects of life on the land may seem to be disproved by evidence which can be collected from the study of the peasant populations or farmers or farm labourers of today. It may be argued that these people are not of such quality as to make it appear that life on the land is the best life and produces the finest type, mentally or physically.

There are two main answers to that argument. The first is that before accepting or rejecting it, the criteria by which men are judged should be closely defined and examined, so that less obtrusive merits may not be undervalued in comparison with more flashy ones. The second answer is more direct, and is to the effect that the people now on the land are a residue in a way of life which for very many years has been the least regarded, the least favored, the least understood of all the ways of life open to man. There has been every temptation for people of enterprise, ability, and ambition born on the land to leave it at the earliest opportunity. The marvel really is that there should be people of quality (not in the conventional sense of that word) left on the land at all, as there most certainly are. The underlying facts can therefore be held to support the present arguments rather than to refute them. If, in the course of time, it came about that the attractiveness in the rigidly economic sense of life on the land were at least equal, on the average, to that of industrial or city life, the source of supply for its population would, for that reason if for no other, no longer tend to comprise a high proportion of the less effective members of society, as it does now.

It may therefore be well to summarize the general advantages to the nation of having many people on the land. For the people actually on the land (who are the lucky ones) they include a healthy active physical life; no day spent without fresh air and muscular activity, with access to foods of absolute freshness. Yet this life need not be, under good economic conditions and with reasonable aid from machinery, so strenuous and hard as to be exhausting, as it often has to be nowadays. Not only physically is the life ideal. It provides unlimited material for man to sharpen his wits on. There is no possible end to the interest and even excitement to be derived from it. All but the very simplest jobs demand the exercise of skill, responsibility, and decision. There is opportunity for the exercise of craftsmanship up to the point at which it merges into art. Rarely need two days be the same. Two seasons are never so. To the man with half an eye it need never be dull.

The spiritual value of contact with reality, of feeling oneself part of nature, like all the most valuable things, is not statistically measurable, but is no less real for that. Close contact with living things brings a kind of wisdom not always appreciated by those to whom such things are unfamiliar, to whom in fact it often appears as a kind of slowness. This wisdom comes through a gradual absorption, usually unaccompanied by conscious realization or power to put into words, of the principles which govern the behavior of living things, of which man is but one.

There must always be many people not actually living on the land. These should have the advantage of being able to consume a far greater proportion than they can today of home-grown foods, fresh and of good quality. They should have a large rural market for their industrial products. It might be possible for a considerable number of them to spend a part of their lives on the land; indeed this might be the most advantageous kind of arrangement for all concerned. Under a rational economy, the present urge of concentration of population into huge masses would cease to be felt, and industry might well be more distributed and actually less physically separated from agriculture than it is at present. Whether this were so or no, the interests of town dwellers could not fail to be more directed to the land, owing to more frequent and close family and commercial relationships. The outlook of education would probably undergo a corresponding change. A real community of interest would be established from which town and country dwellers would derive equal benefit. It may not be unreasonable to envisage a renaissance of direct marketing: produce from neighboring farms being brought in for direct sale in towns, and townspeople going out into the country to buy their food. The extent to which such changes could develop is unlimited. Any move in the right direction is to be encouraged.

Townspeople will probably outnumber country people in the British Isles for a long time to come. Even today they are more and more claiming a right to a share in the pleasures the country can afford but not in its toils. There is today an apparent opposition of town and country which must not be accentuated. Any picture of the future is very incomplete if it appears that everything is to be run for the benefit of the farmer, and that the townsman's gain is to be at best indirect, through a better quality of his food, a better market for his goods—and a few more country cousins!

There is no reason why this should be so. Most districts have considerable areas of land more or less unsuitable for anything approaching high-class farming, which could either be reserved as public parks and playgrounds, or used solely as grazing areas in conjunction with neighboring lands more highly farmed, or as woods. To such lands the public should have free access, and in certain parts of the country it might be worthwhile reserving for such purposes land which otherwise could advantageously be highly cultivated, provided that all the rest were developed to the full. Thus we can help fulfill the ideal of diversification, so essential to vitality.

Apart, however, from special provision for town dwellers, to an educated eye what is more pleasant than the spectacle of a smiling and prosperous countryside? It is more deeply satisfying than the wildest and most romantic scenery, or the most perfectly designed and cared-for park. Its aesthetic appeal is rooted in some of our deepest instincts. The present-day townsman's view of the country is distorted, not only by its not providing a picture of abundant life and prosperity for him to feast his eyes on; not only by his lack of understanding of its life, and of the inherent beauty of the process of the conversion of ordure into use and life, but also by his entirely lamentable feeling that his interests appear to be opposed to those of the countryman. Hence his lack of respect for the elementary and by no means troublesome courtesies of the countryside—such as shutting gates and not smashing fences—which accentuates the lack of sympathy between him and the countryman. With a growth of mutual sympathy and understanding based on a real community of interests most of the existing reasons for the farmer's suspicion and dislike of hikers and 'trespassers' would disappear.

It is conceivable that real sympathy and understanding could be established even though the industrial population should continue to be concentrated mainly in very large towns, as at present. How much better for them and every one else it would be that they should be better distributed; that a far bigger proportion at least of the population should live in villages or small towns, acting as civic, social, and economic centers for the country immediately surrounding them. Socially, even today, the village is a living unit in which most of the people know each other; the large town is socially a desert, the home of individual and class isolation, having no single social life of its own. Indeed, unless some dispersion took place, the full harmony of agriculture, industry, culture, and social life could never reach its full possibility. Anyone who from love of the country fears that this means universal urbanization should look at it the other way round. It is intended to mean a real ruralization, including possibilities of cultural development of the highest order. Few people have seen this more clearly than Mr Trislan Edwards, originator of the 'Hundred New Towns' scheme, which is very fully worked out and exhibits a remarkable combination of vision and practicality.

All this implies a greatly decentralized civic responsibility, based on an organic upward growth, not on delegation from some artificially conceived authority, entrusted with an impossible task of 'planning' or 'organizing'. For no human mind can grasp as a comprehensible or manageable whole the interrelations of more than a few living units. The same does not necessarily apply to non-living units, though it may do so, as in the case of an automatic telephone exchange, which is built up of units of about 200 connections each, that being the greatest number which can be strung together coherently by human ingenuity. The resulting units can then be treated as single phenomena, and strung together to form yet higher and more complex units, which work although no man can grasp the whole of their working.

Therefore, if we are to have any kind of human rule (and we are not likely to be able to dispense with something of the kind for some time yet) it can only be based on the existence of sound primary units, in themselves coherent and self-contained, which can be built up into larger units, in their turn coherent and self-contained. They cannot be coherent and self-contained unless they are so in the biological sense, which includes and comprehends all possible social, political, and economic aspects. We have seen that a farm, to be healthy, must be not too big, yet must be diversified so as to be as far as possible biologically self-contained. Our society must be built up on that very foundation, and it must take the same form for the same reasons. Only thus can the world of life produce a true surplus, an increase of wealth which is real in that it exists not on paper or in the imagination alone, in that it is primarily qualitative, and in that it includes the spiritual values with the material values as incidentals only. All the ingenuity and goodwill in the world expended on industrial or political organization in the modern sense must be in vain if this primary need is not realized.

Organization is anyhow an odious word. It implies all the wrong things. We have tried to organize the soil, and we find that we have destroyed in it the property that matters most—its natural structure. Those who by their own efforts or by chance have acquired social power are doing exactly the same thing to human society—often, of course, with the best intentions; but failure seems to be inevitable.

This leads to the consideration of the part which government must play if the structure of human society is to be rebuilt on a surer foundation. The short answer is that the main function of government must be the administration for the public good of two rights which must be vested in the Crown: the right to occupy land and the right to issue money. Neglect of this principle has contributed largely to the development of a situation in which the government finds itself increasingly compelled to take over the administration of almost everything else; in which State Socialism in one of its many forms is forced on the community because private economic dictatorship becomes intolerable, and eventually governmental political dictatorship appears to be the only alternative, in the absence of a sound social-biological structure in society, such as would make a more rational form of government possible. The authority of government must be built up again from below, so that by the time the top is reached a manageable task is presented. To complete the fantasy of the present position, the present unmanageable task of government is usually supposed to be exercised at the behest, or under the direction, of the majority of individual voters, who are supposed to be educated to understand what they are voting about, though the question on which the vote is taken may be one of foreign policy, the comprehension of which would necessitate the ability to grasp as a whole the situation of the entire world. No living person can approach, let alone attain, such a grasp, in the present structureless state of society. On the other hand a society with a balanced structure would of itself exhibit comprehensible characteristics, peculiar to itself. They would not be comparable to the characteristics of individuals, but would have their own nature, to be studied as such; just as the behavior of a complex organism cannot by any means be inferred from a summation of the characteristics of its constituent cells. Yet the organism can be studied as a whole, and, as a result of such study, its behavior in particular circumstances can be predicted.

The government can do but little to promote the growth of an organic wholeness in society. In its absence, even the taking over by the government of the administration of land and money might do little good, and might even do harm. It might only mean the substitution of an inhuman landlord or banker for a human, and therefore at least sometimes an understanding one. It is in fact difficult to see how much real improvement can come about until people cease to expect anything whatever of the government, and consider instead how they can make themselves, and then their neighborhood, most independent of it. Unfortunately with the increase of governmental responsibility, exercised as it is through so many channels, and with the prevalent increase of taxation, the limits within which any social independence can be achieved are constantly being narrowed. But we can begin anywhere on the land to work for some degree of biological independence. There is the chance.

It is impossible to foresee how the change may come about; but come it must. We may, if we like, amuse ourselves by imagining a parliament of the future concerned chiefly with the administration of land and money, with the first object of encouraging a sound biological development of the country, with a passion for diversification and a deep loathing and mistrust of organization and of legislation in all its forms. But to do so will not lead us far, as our thoughts will be starting from the top and not from the bottom. We can only hope that the British genius for adaptation may be allowed to effect all necessary changes as it were imperceptibly, and without hurry. We must feel our way from a proper care of the land to higher things. The land must be the starting-point, so perhaps those who are in a position to influence the treatment of even a small bit of it have the greatest responsibility. Out of their efforts must come that new thing which will not be like anything known before: a new wholeness or harmony in the world of life, which is now so broken up and divided against itself. Man's strife against man is merely an incidental part of a world-embracing disharmony, the full nature of which is probably still obscure, though its effects can be traced in every department of human life. We must see—or feel—it as a whole, not only in its separate effects. When we can do that, the way out will be clear.

We still habitually look at life in bits and pieces; we analyze and specialize in all departments and are completely bewildered by the complexity of the results. We try to tackle each bit separately; our doing so invariably produces a complication somewhere else. The Hydra grows two heads for each one we cut off. We can never correct even our diet bit by bit. But the conception of a whole diet is a simple one; remembering that 'whole' means both healthy and complete. If we can see life as a whole, we must also be able to see that we cannot have a whole diet unless the creatures on which we depend have one. Not the least important of those creatures (perhaps) are the microscopic ones in the soil. On their vitality depends ours, and on our vitality depends theirs. For we must farm or die. In undertaking farming we undertake a responsibility covering the whole life cycle. We can break it or keep it whole. We have broken it, but there is yet time to mend it; perhaps only just time.

The nature of living things is that they are not mere machines. The fact that from one point of view they are machines has largely deceived us. But they are something more. That something more does not respond to mechanical or statistical treatment. It responds only to that for which we have no other word but love. Love can express itself in many ways, but if it is genuine it means giving—not of gifts but of self. We have tried to get without giving more than we could help. 'Give and you shall receive' is not sentimental idealism, it is a simple, practical rule. That which we can and must give to the land is work, and if that work is given in love it will not be drudgery. But it will and must be work. The so-called 'curse of Adam' is upon us: 'By the sweat of your brow you shall eat bread.' Has it not become obvious that if we try to avoid it we die? But why call it a curse? Why not welcome it as a clue to our rejuvenation in terms of natural life? That kind of rejuvenation seems to be a necessary part of the rejuvenation of the life of the spirit for which every human being worthy of the name so ardently longs.

If we are to succeed in the great task before us we must adopt a humbler attitude towards the elementary things of life than that which is implied in our frequent boasting about our so-called 'Conquest of Nature'. We have put ourselves on a pinnacle in the pride of an imagined conquest. But we cannot separate ourselves from nature if we would. The idea of conquering nature is as sensible as if a man should try to cut off his own head so as to isolate his superior faculties. There can be no quarrel between ourselves and nature any more than there can be a quarrel between a man's head and his feet. If such a quarrel is invented it is the man who suffers, including both his head and his feet. We have invented or imagined a fight between ourselves and nature; so of course the whole of nature, which includes ourselves as well as the soil, suffers. We have even come to regard nature as something primitive, terrible, and squalid. If she is so, it is we who have made her so.

Nature is only terrible or squalid to those who do not understand her, and when misunderstanding has upset her balance. She is imbued above all with the power of love; by love she can after all be conquered, but in no other way. That has not been our way. We have attempted a less excellent way, and have upset the 'balance of nature', so that she no longer appears to us in pleasant guise but in a guise in which the appearance of an opposition of forces—a 'struggle for existence'—predominates over the appearance of a balance of forces. So we have come to believe in a struggle for existence as the only possibility, and we infer that any such struggle is necessarily painful. It is painful now, and not only to ourselves. But it was not always so and need not always be so. We are the head and have the responsibility. We have tried to conquer nature by force and by intellect. It now remains for us to try the way of love.

Printed in the United States
49762LVS00006B/3